Teacher's Pres...

 Corrective Mathematics

Basic
Fractions $\frac{1}{2}$

Siegfried Engelmann • Don Steely

Columbus, OH

The *McGraw·Hill* Companies

SRAonline.com

 SRA

Copyright © 2005 by SRA/McGraw-Hill.

All rights reserved. Except as permitted under the
United States Copyright Act, no part of this publication
may be reproduced or distributed in any form or by any
means, or stored in a database or retrieval system,
without the prior written permission of the publisher,
unless otherwise indicated.

Send all inquiries to:
SRA/McGraw-Hill
8787 Orion Place
Columbus, OH 43240-4027

Printed in the United States of America.

ISBN 0-07-602473-3

1 2 3 4 5 6 7 8 9 MAL 09 08 07 06 05

The McGraw-Hill Companies

Contents

Contents (continued)

The Presentation

The Guide

The Program

Corrective Mathematics consists of seven modules:

- Addition
- Subtraction
- Multiplication
- Division
- Basic Fractions
- Fractions, Decimals, and Percents
- Ratios and Equations

Components for each module of **Corrective Mathematics** include:

- Teacher's Presentation Book
- consumable Workbook
- Answer Key

Corrective Mathematics Comprehensive Placement Test in the *Series Guide* identifies which modules the students need. The modules can be used separately or in combination. They can be presented to entire classes, small instructional groups, or individual students.

Basic Fractions is a modular program to teach beginning fraction skills. It can be followed by *Fractions, Decimals, and Percents.* By the end of *Basic Fractions,* the students will be able to:

- Add and subtract fractions and mixed numbers with common denominators
- Multiply fractions, whole numbers, and mixed numbers
- Convert some fractions to numbers (such as $\frac{6}{6}, \frac{18}{1}, \frac{48}{6}$) and numbers to fractions ($5 = \frac{5}{1}$)
- Tell whether a fraction is more than, less than, or equal to 1
- Convert mixed numbers to fractions
- Find equivalent fractions ($\frac{2}{3} = \frac{}{18}$)

Basic Fractions is designed to be taught every day. There are 55 lessons. Each lesson takes approximately 20 minutes. *Basic Fractions* can be taught simultaneously with other skills, such as long division or column multiplication.

The program is for any student who cannot work fraction problems but who knows (a) basic addition and subtraction facts and (b) multiplication facts through the 6s. It can be used as a remedial program or as an introductory program.

Materials

The materials for *Basic Fractions* include this *Teacher's Presentation Book*, a *Workbook* for each student, and an *Answer Key.*

The *Workbook* contains daily worksheets, a Five-Lesson Point Graph, and Five-Lesson Point Summaries. For most lessons there is only one workbook page.

The *Teacher's Presentation Book* contains day-by-day lessons and information about placement, starting the program, awarding points, recording points, teaching the program, and modifying the program.

The *Teacher's Presentation Book* contains a script for each lesson. Scripts specify what you say and do and what the students say and do.

- This type indicates what you say.
- (This type indicates what you do.)
- *This italic type indicates the students' response.*

Placement Procedure

Pretest

The pretest is at the back of this book, and it may be reproduced. The pretest should be administered to each student before placement in *Basic Fractions.*

There are two parts to the pretest. Part 1 helps you determine whether the student can begin work in *Basic Fractions.* If the student can begin work in *Basic Fractions,* Part 2 of the pretest will help you determine where the student should begin.

Administration of Pretest

The pretest may be given as a group test or as an individual test. First give Part 1 to determine which students can begin work in *Basic Fractions.* Give Part 2 of the pretest to all students who can work in the program.

Have each student write their name at the top of the test form.

> a. (Tell the students to touch the first problem in Part 1. Check to make sure the students are pointing to the correct problem.)
> b. You have two minutes to work the addition problems in Part A. Work fast, but try not to make mistakes.
> c. (Stop students after two minutes.)
> d. (Repeat this procedure with Parts B and C.)

The same procedures are used for Part 2 of the pretest—allow two minutes for each section.

Part 1—Placement

Grade Part 1 of the pretest and record the errors for each section on the Pretest Error Chart. The Pretest Error Chart is at the back of this book.

Name	Errors					
	A	**B**	**C**	**D**	**E**	**F**
Bob	5	4	2			
Tamiko	1	0	5			
Daley	3	4	8			
Lisa	7	4	15			

- If the student did not make more than 5 errors on any test, the student my start work in *Basic Fractions.* In the sample error chart at the bottom of the first column, Bob and Tamiko qualify for placement in *Basic Fractions.*
- If the student did not make more than 5 errors in either Part A or Part B, but made 6 to 10 errors in Part C, the student may begin *Basic Fractions.* However, the student must have additional work on multiplication facts up through the 6s. (See Daley's scores.) Multiplying fractions does not begin until Lesson 24, so there are five weeks to review multiplication facts.
- If the student made more that 5 errors in Part A or B, or more than 10 errors in Part C, the student needs more work on facts before beginning the program. (Lisa fits these criteria.) The ***Corrective Mathematics*** Comprehensive Placement Test in the *Series Guide* identifies which modules the student needs.

> **Note:** By Lesson 37, students must know addition facts through sums of 20, subtraction facts that do not involve borrowing through 19-minus-a-number, and all multiplication facts through the 10s. If the students do not know these facts, begin working on them now so the students will be able to work the problems in Lesson 37–55.

Part 2—Placement

Grade Part 2 of the pretest and record the errors for each section on the Pretest Error Chart.

- If the student made more than 1 error in Part D, the student should begin on Lesson 1.
- If the student made 1 or fewer errors in Part D, but more than 1 error in Part E, the student should begin on Lesson 20.
- If the student made 1 or fewer errors in Part D and 1 or fewer errors in Part E, but more than 1 error in Part F, the student should begin on Lesson 30.

- If the student made 1 or fewer errors in each of the Parts D, E, or F, the student should not be placed in *Basic Fractions*. Use the pretest for *Fractions, Decimals, and Percents* for appropriate placement.

Basic Fractions can be taught individually or to groups of students. If you are teaching *Basic Fractions* to more than ten students, it is best to group the students. This will allow the faster students to progress through the program more rapidly because certain lessons can be skipped. This is explained in the Modifying the Program section of this book.

Group the students according to their pretest scores. Put those students with the fewest total pretest errors in a faster group. Correspondingly, put the students with the most pretest errors in the slowest group. Ideal group size is between seven and ten.

Starting the Program

Before you begin the program, set aside a time for meeting with those students who will be in the program. This meeting is important for establishing a positive attitude toward what is going to happen and how it is going to happen. Students might have negative attitudes toward math, perhaps expressing the idea that something is wrong with them. During the initial meeting with the students, make these points clear:

1. The fact that these students are poor in mathematics is not an indication that they are not intelligent.

2. The only reason these students have trouble with math is that no one really taught them how to work the problems.

3. You are going to teach them to do the problems, but you do not have any magic way of doing it. You are responsible for working very hard to teach them, and they are responsible for working hard to learn.

Briefly describe the general rules about what the students will be doing during each lesson.

- They will work on fractions each day for about 20 minutes.
- When you ask questions, they will respond as a group unless you call on an individual.
- They will do the problems on their worksheets, according to your instructions.

Awarding Points

Emphasize that:

1. The students earn daily points based on individual performance on worksheet items. Students can earn as many as 10 points by making no more than 2 errors on a daily worksheet.

2. Every student in the group earns up to 5 additional points for hard work in each lesson if the group works hard and answers on signal.

3. Students may be awarded bonus points for work on particular skills as you decide it is needed.

4. Grades are based on the number of points earned during the grading period. If students average 50 points or more for five-lesson totals, they receive an A.

The next topic of the initial meeting should be behavioral rules. Here is a sample set of behavioral rules for a math class:

1. Watch the teacher.

2. Answer when the teacher signals.

3. Sit quietly when you finish your work.

The important considerations in formulating behavioral rules are (a) state the rules prior to instruction, (b) use as few rules as possible to cover anticipated problem behavior, (c) make the rules positive, and (d) keep the rules simple. Other rules might include regular attendance, bringing a pencil to class, and encouraging fellow students to do good work.

Bonus points may be used to deal with behaviors not anticipated in advance. For instance, if tardiness becomes a problem you might offer 2 bonus points to everyone who is ready to work when class starts.

Recording Points ●————————

Basic Fractions has daily points forms and summary point forms. These forms allow the students to see their progress each day from the beginning of the program.

The last task in each lesson is a Workcheck. After the students have exchanged workbooks, checked the answers, and returned the workbooks, each student records the points at the top of the workbook page. The students then turn to the **Point Summary Charts,** and write the points in the appropriate box.

Lesson	1	2	3	4	5	Total
Points						

The point chart below and at the back of the *Workbook* tells the students how many points are received for a given number of errors. Group points and "Hard Work" points are given, and the students can add their points for the lessons, and write the number in the total points box. At the end of each five-lesson period, the students add up their total points for the five-lesson period and record the total in the box labeled Total.

Daily Points

Daily points will be awarded by the teacher as follows:

1. **Worksheet Items**

Errors	Points
0–2	10
3	7
4	5
5	3
6	1
7 or more	0

2. **Hard Work** 0–5 group points for working hard and answering on signal. Everyone in the group will receive the same number of points for oral work.

Five-Lesson Point Graph

The **Five-Lesson Point Graph** at the back of the *Workbook* shows progress for each five-lesson interval. It is filled out only once every five lessons to provide the students with a graphic display of their performance. To chart performance on the graph, the students record the five-lesson point total below the appropriate five-lesson group at the bottom of the graph. Then they make a bar graph of the total. The top of the bar is aligned to the appropriate number of points in the left column.

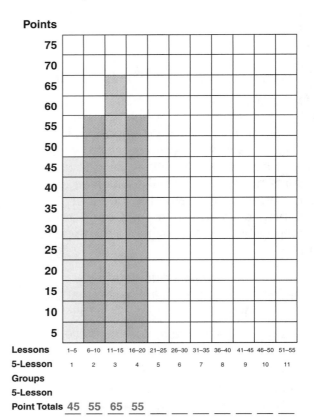

Lessons	1–5 6–10 11–15 16–20 21–25 26–30 31–35 36–40 41–45 46–50 51–55	
5-Lesson Groups	1 2 3 4 5 6 7 8 9 10 11	
5-Lesson Point Totals	45 55 65 55 __ __ __ __ __ __ __	

Letter Grades

Grades can be computed for any period of time by averaging the five-lesson point totals and awarding grades accordingly.

A grade   The average of five-lesson totals is at least 50 points.

B grade   The average of five-lesson totals is 40–49 points.

C grade   The average of five-lesson totals is 30–39 points.

Summary of Recording Procedure

1. Instruct students to record points earned in the "Items" box at the top of the worksheet.

2. As soon as the worksheet "Items" points have been determined, award the points for group "Hard Work." Your criterion should be based on whether the group apparently tried, attended, and responded.
   You did a good job today. Everyone gets 4 points for hard work. Write 4 for "Hard Work."

3. Award any applicable bonus points as part of "Hard Work."

4. Have students total their points and record their total points for the lesson in the appropriate box at the top of their worksheets.

5. Ask students to turn to the Point Summary Charts at the back of their books and record the number of points earned on the chart.

6. At the end of every fifth lesson, have the students figure their five-lesson point total and plot it on the Five-Lesson Point Graph.

7. Grades may be computed at any time. If grades are to be given after six weeks, for instance, simply add up the five-lesson totals for the first six weeks and divide that number by 6. Assign grades.

When properly awarded, grades work as strong reinforcers of good social and academic behavior. But the strongest potential reinforcer is success. This program is designed so that the student will have success and will be fully aware of it.

Teaching the Program

The *Teacher's Presentation Book* contains daily lessons. Each lesson will involve some board work and some worksheet exercises. The board work is presented by the teacher and is used to teach the students new concepts and skills. The worksheets are used to practice and strengthen skills.

Each lesson in the *Teacher's Presentation Book* is laid out in the same way.

EXERCISE 3

Addition/Subtraction

a. (Draw on the board:)
★
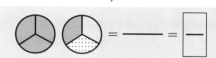

- We're going to write the fraction for this picture. We're going to use a plus sign to show the different parts.
- How many parts are in each whole? (Signal.) *3.*
- So, I'll write a 3 on the bottom.
- (Write to show:)

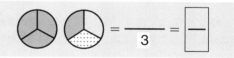

b. Some of the parts that are used are shaded and some are dotted. Count all the shaded parts. (Pause.)
- How many parts are shaded? (Signal.) *4.*
- So, I'll write a 4 on the top.
- (Write to show:)

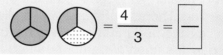

c. Now I'm going to add the parts that are dotted, so I write a plus sign.

- (Write to show:)

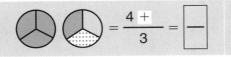

- Count all the dotted parts.
- How many parts are dotted? (Signal.) *1.*

- The heading tells what skill the students are working on.
- This type indicates what you say.
- (This type indicates what you do.)
- *This italic type indicates the students' response.*
- A check mark (✔) indicates when you quickly check that students are on task.

The Setup

Seats should be arranged so that the front row of students is immediately in front of you as you stand at the board. If the group is very large, consider using a portable board to avoid moving chairs and desks. You will write on the board as you teach the lesson.

Arrange the seating to insure that low performers are seated near you and potential behavior-problem students are not sitting next to each other. Students should have their *Workbooks.*

Signals

Students must give their responses to exercises as a group when you give a signal. The use of signals and group responses insures that every student is getting adequate practice in responding. The use of signals also allows you to monitor the performance of each student in the group. If students are not required to respond in unison—some coming in early, some late, and some not at all—some students might simply copy the responses of others, and you will not get adequate feedback on student performance. When the program is presented in a positive manner and the teacher treats

responding to signals as a very important convention, students of all ages adapt very well to group response on signal.

Here are the rules for effective signaling.

1. Never signal while you are talking. Talk first, and then signal.

2. The time interval between the last word of your instructions and the signal should always be about one second. Signals should be timed so that students can respond together.

The hand-drop signal is used for tasks that you present orally. Follow these steps to execute this signal.

1. Hold your hand out (as if you're stopping traffic) while you are saying the instructions or presenting the question.

2. Continue to hold your hand still for one second after you have completed the instructions or the question.

3. Then quickly drop your hand. Students should respond the instant your hand drops.

Corrections

All students will make mistakes. These mistakes provide you with valuable information about the difficulties the students are having. Knowing how to correct effectively is essential to successful teaching.

Mistakes should be corrected immediately. Some correction procedures are included in the Presentation. (They are enclosed in ▶ ◀ and titled "To Correct.") When there is no correction in the Presentation section, two other kinds of correction procedures are used—general corrections and specific corrections. These are explained below.

General Corrections. If a student is not paying attention during an exercise, correct by looking at the nonattender and saying:

Watch me and listen. Let's try it again.

Then return to the beginning of the task.

If a student fails to answer when you give the signal, correct by saying:

I have to hear everybody. Let's try it again.

Then return to the beginning of the task.

If a student responds either before or too long after your signal, call attention to the signal and return to the beginning of the exercise. For example, if students respond before you signal, say:

You've got to wait until I signal. Let's try it again.

Specific Corrections. Other mistakes that students will make involve not knowing the correct answers to an exercise you present.

When student's don't know the correct answer to a question you present, correct with the following procedure.

1. Tell students that their answer is wrong. If necessary, tell them the answer.
2. Repeat the step.
3. Provide a delayed test by returning to the beginning of the task in which the mistake occurred and presenting the steps in order.
4. To correct persistent mistakes, present similar exercises, which usually can be found in earlier lessons.

Pacing

Each lesson in *Basic Fractions* contains many exercises. Therefore, each exercise must be taught quickly, but not so quickly as to rush the students into making errors. Never rush to finish a lesson in the allotted time. On some exercises, the students need time to think or time to count. You have to pause to give the students that time. Places where you must pause are marked like this: (Pause.) Pause for three to six seconds whenever you see the pause sign.

To keep the lesson from dragging, familiarize yourself with each lesson so that it is not necessary to read each exercise word for word during the presentation.

Checking

It is important to make sure that the lower performing students are working a problem correctly or that they are writing the problem the correct way. Places where this is important are marked with a check mark (✔). If the lower performing students are placed near you, it is not difficult to walk around and check their work.

In general, it is a good practice to walk around and check all students when they are working on their worksheet exercises. Spend most of the time with the lower performing students.

Worksheets

During each lesson, a skill will first be taught or reviewed on the board, and then the students will do similar problems on their worksheets. This procedure will be repeated several times during each lesson. Make sure the students do not go ahead and work other problems.

Each section of the worksheet is timed. The students have a certain number of minutes to finish each part before you continue with more board work. For most students, the indicated time will be sufficient. If all students finish a section early, proceed with the next exercise. If most of the students need a little more time, wait before proceeding. The time limits are there to keep the students from plodding and to keep the lesson under 20 minutes. You may be flexible as needed.

If only a few students do not finish a section when the time is up, go on with the next exercise. Later in the day, give those students who did not finish enough time to complete each section. If this is a persistent occurrence, you might want to do the previous lesson's workcheck at the beginning the period so all students may grade their worksheets at the same time.

After the students have finished working a section on their worksheets, have them put their pencils down before you begin doing the board work for the next exercise.

If the lessons are taught as specified, the student will have a few worksheet errors. If for any reason, the students make a great number of errors, you will have to repeat the lesson. If 1 fourth of the students make more than 10 errors, repeat the entire lesson to the entire class on the next day. This will necessitate making new worksheets for each student. Do not proceed until the students are below the error rate. If you proceed without repeating the lessons, the students will have difficulty with succeeding lessons.

Workchecks

At the end of each lesson is a workcheck. The students exchange workbooks and check the answers as you read them. Walk around the room during the workcheck to make sure that everyone is marking wrong answers.

After the students have returned their workbooks, they will fill out their charts. During the first few lessons, help the students through the procedure for recording errors, determining points, and totaling points. After the first five days, it should not be necessary to help the students complete their charts. However, it is a good idea to occasionally collect student workbooks and check to make sure that the students are giving themselves the correct number of points.

Conventions

Throughout the program, fractions are written like this: $\frac{6}{7}$. Do not use the diagonal line (6/7).

If you want to teach the diagonal notation to the students, do so after Lesson 55.

In Lessons 1–16, the students are learning the names of fractions with denominators of halves through tenths. In these lessons, they will be reading many of the fractions as *6 over 7* for $\frac{6}{7}$.

In Lessons 1–16, they may read the fractions by their common names (6 sevenths), but do not insist that they do. After Lesson 16, all fractions are ready by their common names.

After Lesson 36, some fractions will have denominators greater than 10. Most students will be able to read these fractions even though the fractions have not been taught. If students have any difficulty reading the larger denominator fractions, tell them how to say the fractions, have them read the fraction two times, and proceed with the lesson. Do not make a big issue about reading big denominator fractions.

Modifying the Program

Most students will find the program easy—*Basic Fractions* was designed that way. However, some students might not need the amount of practice and review that are provided in the program. They may skip some lessons. At the beginning of certain lessons, a skipping note will appear. Students may skip a lesson if: *no more than 1 fourth of the students missed more than 4 problems.*

When a lesson is skipped, the students should get the full 10 points for their worksheet. The lessons that may be skipped *if the criterion is met are:* 5, 7, 16, 18, 24, 26, 32, 38, 44, 49. In Lessons **5** and **7,** the common names of some fractions are introduced. In these lessons, the group may skip everything **except the exercise named Fraction Naming.** When skipping Lessons 5 and 7, first do the Fraction Naming exercise and then proceed to the next lesson. For the other "skip" lessons, you may skip the entire lesson.

The Presentation

Lesson 1

- (Post the following information:)

Worksheet Items	Errors	Points
	0–2	10
	3	7
	4	5
	5	3
	6	1
	7 or more	0

- (Students will refer to it during each lesson.)

EXERCISE 1

Fraction Rule

a. Here is a rule about fractions. The bottom number of a fraction tells how many parts in each whole. Listen again. The bottom number of a fraction tells how many parts in each whole.

b. What does the bottom number of a fraction tell? (Signal.) *How many parts in each whole.*

▶ **To Correct**
(Repeat steps a and b.) ◀

c. Again, what does the bottom number of a fraction tell? (Signal.) *How many parts in each whole.*
- (Repeat until all students can say the rule.

d. (Write on the board:)

$$\frac{}{4}$$

- This number tells 4 parts in each whole. What does this number tell? (Signal.) *4 parts in each whole.*

e. (Change to show:)

$$\frac{}{6}$$

- What does this number tell? (Signal.) *6 parts in each whole.*

f. (Repeat step e for $\dfrac{}{2}$ $\dfrac{}{5}$ $\dfrac{}{3}$.)

★**Option:** Draw diagram before starting the lesson.

EXERCISE 2

Denominator Counting

a. (Draw on the board:)
★

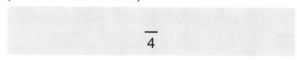

b. (Point to each circle and say:) This is a whole.

c. Let's figure out how many parts are in each whole. I'll touch the parts, and you count them. Get ready.
- (Touch each part in the first whole as the students count.) *1, 2, 3, 4.*

d. How many parts in this whole? (Signal.) *4.*

e. I'll touch the parts in the next whole. You count the parts. Get ready.
- (Touch each part in the second whole as the students count.) *1, 2, 3, 4.*

f. How many parts in this whole? (Signal.) *4.*

g. Let's count the parts in the next whole. Get ready.
- (Touch each part in the third whole as the students count.) *1, 2, 3, 4.*

h. How many parts in this whole? (Signal.) *4.*

i. How many parts in each whole? (Signal.) *4.*

j. What's the bottom number of a fraction tell? (Signal.) *How many parts in each whole.*

k. So where do I write the 4? (Signal.) *On the bottom.*

▶ **To Correct**

1. What does the bottom number of a fraction tell? (Signal.) *How many parts in each whole.*

2. There are 4 parts in each whole. So where do I write the 4? (Signal.) *On the bottom.* ◀

l. (Write to show:)

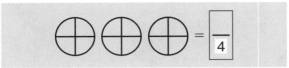

New Problem

a. (Draw on the board:)

★

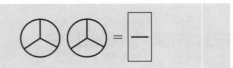

b. Let's figure out how many parts are in each whole. I'll touch the parts, and you count them. Get ready.
- (Touch each part in the first whole as the students count.) *1, 2, 3.*
c. How many parts in this whole? (Signal.) *3.*
d. I'll touch the parts in the next whole. You count the parts. Get ready.
- (Touch each part in the second whole as the students count.) *1, 2, 3.*
e. How many parts in this whole? (Signal.) *3.*
f. How many parts are there in each whole? (Signal.) *3.*
g. What does the bottom number of a fraction tell? (Signal.) *How many parts in each whole.*
h. So where do I write the 3? (Signal.) *On the bottom.*
i. (Write to show:)

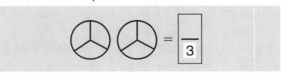

New Problem

a. (Draw on the board:)

★

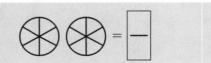

b. Let's figure out how many parts are in each whole. I'll touch the parts, and you count them. Get ready.
- (Touch each part in the first whole as the students count.) *1, 2, 3, 4, 5, 6.*
c. How many parts in this whole? (Signal.) *6.*
d. I'll touch the parts in the next whole. You count the parts. Get ready.
- (Touch each part in the second whole as the students count.) *1, 2, 3, 4, 5, 6.*
e. How many parts in this whole? (Signal.) *6.*
f. How many parts are there in each whole? (Signal.) *6.*
g. What does the bottom number of a fraction tell? (Signal.) *How many parts in each whole.*
h. So where do I write the 6? (Signal.) *On the bottom.*
i. (Write to show:)

Workbook Practice

a. Turn to Lesson 1 in your workbook. Find Part 1. ✔
- Touch the first problem. ✔
- You have to figure out how many parts are in each whole. Count to yourself. Figure out how many parts in the first whole. (Pause.)
- How many parts are in the first whole? (Signal.) *4.*
b. Count to yourself. Figure out how many parts are in the next whole. (Pause.)
- How many parts in that whole? (Signal.) *4.*
c. How many parts in each whole? (Signal.) *4.*
- Where do you write the 4? (Signal.) *On the bottom.*
- Write the 4. ✔
d. Work the rest of the problems in Part 1 the same way. You have 5 minutes.
- (Observe students and give feedback.)

EXERCISE 3

Workcheck

a. We're going to check the answers.
Exchange workbooks.
Put an **X** next to each item you got wrong.
- (Read the answers for all rows. See **Answer Key**.)
- Return the workbooks.

b. Now we're going to figure out the number of points you've earned for this lesson.
Count the number of items you got wrong in Part 1.

c. (Draw the following on the board:)

Items	Hard Work	Total
☐	+ ☐	= ☐

d. Find the beginning of your worksheet for Lesson 1. ✔
- You are going to write the number of points you earned in the box labeled "Items." It looks like this. (Point to the correct box on the board.)

e. Now we're going to figure out the number of points you've earned for this lesson.
- (Point to the posted information.)

Worksheet Items	Errors	Points
	0–2	10
	3	7
	4	5
	5	3
	6	1
	7 or more	0

f. If you got 0 items wrong, you get 10 points. If you got 1 wrong, you get 10 points. If you got 2 wrong, you get 10 points. If you got 3 wrong, you get 7 points. If you got 4 wrong, you get 5 points. If you got 5 wrong, you get 3 points. If you got 6 wrong, you get 1 point. If you got 7 or more wrong, you get 0 points.

g. How many points do you get if you got 1 item wrong? (Signal.) *10.*
- How many points do you get if you got 4 items wrong? (Signal.) *5.*

- How many points do you get if you got 8 items wrong? (Signal.) *Zero.*

h. Write the number of points you earned in the box labeled "Items."
- (Check to see that students have recorded their points correctly.)

i. (Award "hard work" points as follows:)

Hard Work   0–5 group points for working hard and answering on signal. Everyone in the group will receive the same number of points for hard work.

j. (If you awarded hard work points during the lesson, either for appropriate group behavior or for very good worksheet performance, say:) Once again find the beginning of your worksheet for Lesson 1.
- You are going to write the number of points you earned in the box labeled "Hard Work." It looks like this. (Point to the correct box on the board.)

k. (You might want to write numbers in the boxes on the board and demonstrate this next step:)
Add up all of the points in the boxes and put the answer in the box labeled "Total." This is the number of points you earned for this lesson.
(During the beginning lessons of this module, you might need to help students total their points.)

l. Turn to the Point Summary Charts on the inside back cover of your workbook. ✔
Find the empty box below Lesson 1. Write the total number of points you earned in that box. ✔
- (Teacher reference from back of *Workbook:*)

Lesson	1	2	3	4	5	Total
Points						

EXERCISE 1

Fraction Rule

a. Remember the rule about fractions. The bottom number of a fraction tells how many parts in each whole. Listen again. The bottom number of a fraction tells how many parts in each whole.

b. What does the bottom number of a fraction tell? (Signal.) *How many parts in each whole.*

c. Again, what does the bottom number of a fraction tell? (Signal.) *How many parts in each whole.*

d. (Write on the board:)

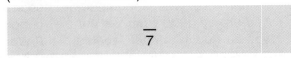

- This number tells 7 parts in each whole. What does this number tell? (Signal.) *7 parts in each whole.*

e. (Change to show:)

- What does this number tell? (Signal.) *9 parts in each whole.*

f. (Repeat step e for $\dfrac{}{8}$ $\dfrac{}{2}$ $\dfrac{}{6}$.)

EXERCISE 2

Denominator Counting

a. (Draw on the board:)
★

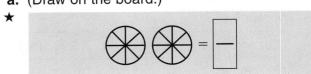

b. (Point to each circle and say:) This is a whole.

c. Let's figure out how many parts are in each whole. I'll touch the parts, and you count them. Get ready.

- (Touch each part in the first whole as the students count.) *1, 2, 3, . . . 8.*

d. How many parts in this whole? (Signal.) *8.*

e. I'll touch the parts in the next whole. You count the parts. Get ready.

- (Touch each part in the second whole as the students count.) *1, 2, 3, . . . 8.*

f. How many parts in this whole? (Signal.) *8.*

g. How many parts are there in each whole? (Signal.) *8.*

h. What does the bottom number of a fraction tell? (Signal.) *How many parts in each whole.*

i. So where do I write the 8? (Signal.) *On the bottom.*

▶ **To Correct**

1. What does the bottom number of a fraction tell? (Signal.) *How many parts in each whole.*

2. There are 8 parts in each whole. So where do I write the 8? (Signal.) *On the bottom.* ◀

j. (Write to show:)

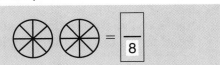

New Problem

a. (Draw on the board:)
★

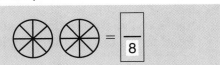

b. (Point to each circle and say:) This is a whole.

c. Let's figure out how many parts are in each whole. I'll touch the parts, and you count them. Get ready.

- (Touch each part in the first whole as the students count.) *1, 2, 3, 4, 5.*

d. How many parts in this whole? (Signal.) *5.*

e. I'll touch the parts in the next whole. You count the parts. Get ready.

- (Touch each part in the second whole as the students count.) *1, 2, 3, 4, 5.*

f. How many parts in this whole? (Signal.) *5.*

g. How many parts are there in each whole? (Signal.) *5.*

h. What does the bottom number of a fraction tell? (Signal.) *How many parts in each whole.*

i. So where do I write the 5? (Signal.) *On the bottom.*

j. (Write to show:)

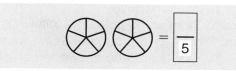

Workbook Practice

a. Turn to Lesson 2 in your workbook. Find Part 1. ✔
- Touch the first problem. ✔
- You have to figure out how many parts are in each whole. Count to yourself. Figure out how many parts are in the first whole. (Pause.)
- How many parts are in the first whole? (Signal.) *5.*

b. Count to yourself. Figure out how many parts are in the next whole. (Pause.)
- How many parts in that whole? (Signal.) *5.*

c. How many parts in each whole? (Signal.) *5.*
- Where do you write the 5? (Signal.) *On the bottom.*
- Write the 5. ✔

d. Work the rest of the problems in Part 1 the same way. You have 4 minutes.
- (Observe students and give feedback.)

EXERCISE 3

Denominator Drawing

a. What does the bottom number of a fraction tell? (Signal.) *How many parts in each whole.*

b. (Write on the board:)

$$\overline{4}$$

- This number tells 4 parts in each whole. What does this number tell? (Signal.) *4 parts in each whole.*

c. (Change to show:)

$$\overline{3}$$

- What does this number tell? (Signal.) *3 parts in each whole.*

d. I'll draw a picture of 3 parts in each whole.
- (Draw 2 circles on the board and divide each into 3 equal parts.)

e. (Touch the first circle.)
- How many parts are in this whole? (Signal.) *3.*

f. (Touch the second circle.)
- How many parts are in this whole? (Signal.) *3.*

g. How many parts in each whole? (Signal.) *3.*

h. Find Part 2 on your worksheet.
- Touch the first problem in Part 2.
- What number is on the bottom of the fraction in the first problem? (Signal.) *4.*

i. What does the 4 tell you? (Signal.) *4 parts in each whole.*

j. Make 4 parts in each whole in the first problem. The first whole is done for you.
- (Observe students and give feedback.)

k. Work the rest of the problems in Part 2 the same way. The bottom number tells how many parts to make in each whole. You have 4 minutes.
- (Observe students and give feedback.)

EXERCISE 4

Workcheck

a. We're going to check the answers. Exchange workbooks. Put an **X** next to each item that the person misses.
- (Check and correct.)
  Part 1
  These are the bottom numbers. Make an **X** next to any number that is not on the bottom. ✔
  Top row: 5, 8, 3, 2.
  Next row: 4, 6, 5, 3.
  Next row: 2, 7, 4, 6.
  Last row: 3, 5, 8, 9.

Part 2

I'll tell you how many equal-sized parts there should be.

Top row: 4, 3, 5, 2.

Next row: 4, 2, 6, 5.

Next row: 2, 6, 4, 3.

Last row: 5, 4, 3, 2.

• Return the workbooks.

b. Now we're going to figure out the number of points you've earned for this lesson.
Count the number of items you got wrong.

c. (Draw the following on the board:)

Items	Hard Work	Total
☐	+ ☐	= ☐

d. Find the beginning of your worksheet for Lesson 2. ✔

• You are going to write the number of points you earned in the box labeled "Items." It looks like this. (Point to the correct box on the board.)

e. Now we're going to figure out the number of points you've earned for this lesson.

• (Point to the posted information.)

Worksheet Items	Errors	Points
	0–2	10
	3	7
	4	5
	5	3
	6	1
	7 or more	0

f. If you got 0 to 2 items wrong, you get 10 points. If you got 3 wrong, you get 7 points. If you got 4 wrong, you get 5 points. If you got 5 wrong, you get 3 points. If you got 6 wrong, you get 1 point. If you got 7 or more wrong, you get 0 points.

g. How many points do you get if you got 2 items wrong? (Signal.) *10.*

• How many points do you get if you got 3 items wrong? (Signal.) *7.*

• How many points do you get if you got 5 items wrong? (Signal.) *3.*

h. Write the number of points you earned in the box labeled "Items."

• (Check to see that students have recorded their points correctly.)

i. (Award "hard work" points as follows:)
Hard Work 0–5 group points for working hard and answering on signal. Everyone in the group will receive the same number of points for hard work.

j. (If you awarded hard work points during the lesson, either for appropriate group behavior or for very good worksheet performance, say:) Once again find the beginning of your worksheet for Lesson 2.

• You are going to write the number of points you earned in the box labeled "Hard Work." It looks like this. (Point to the correct box on the board.)

k. (You might want to write numbers in the boxes on the board and demonstrate this next step:)
Add up all of the points in the boxes and put the answer in the box labeled "Total." This is the number of points you earned for this lesson.
(During the beginning lessons of this module, you might need to help students total their points.)

l. Turn to the Point Summary Charts on the inside back cover of your workbook. ✔
Find the empty box below Lesson 2. Write the total number of points you earned in that box. ✔

EXERCISE 1

Denominator Counting

a. (Draw on the board:)

★
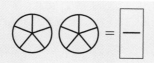

b. Let's figure out how many parts are in each whole. You count them. Get ready.
- (Touch each part in the first whole as the students count.) *1, 2, 3, 4, 5.*
c. Let's count the parts in the next whole. Get ready.
- (Touch each part in the next whole as the students count.) *1, 2, 3, 4, 5.*
- How many parts are there in each whole? (Signal.) *5.*
d. Where do I write the 5? (Signal.) *On the bottom.*
e. (Write to show:)

Workbook Practice

a. Turn to Lesson 3 in your workbook. Find Part 1.
- Touch the first problem in Part 1.
- You have to figure out how many parts are in each whole. Count to yourself. Figure out how many parts are in the first whole. (Pause.)
- How many parts are in the first whole? (Signal.) *6.*
b. Count to yourself. Figure out how many parts are in the next whole? (Pause.)
- How many parts are in the first whole? (Signal.) *6.*
- How many parts are in each whole? (Signal.) *6.*
c. Where do you write the 6? (Signal.) *On the bottom.*
- Write the 6. ✔

d. Work the rest of the problems in Part 1 the same way. You have 4 minutes.
- (Observe students and give feedback.)

EXERCISE 2

Denominator Drawing

a. What does the bottom number of a fraction tell? (Signal.) *How many parts in each whole.*
b. (Write on the board:)

- This number tells 5 parts in each whole. What does this number tell? (Signal.) *5 parts in each whole.*
c. (Change to show:)

- What does this number tell? (Signal.) *2 parts in each whole.*
d. (Touch the fraction.) I'll draw a picture of 2 parts in each whole.
- (Draw 2 circles on the board and divide each into 2 parts.)
e. (Touch the first circle.)
- How many parts in this whole? (Signal.) *2.*
f. (Touch the second circle.)
- How many parts in this whole? (Signal.) *2.*
g. How many parts in each whole? (Signal.) *2.*
h. Find Part 2 on your worksheet.
- Touch the first problem in Part 2. ✔
- What number is on the bottom of the fraction in the first problem? (Signal.) *5.*
i. What does the 5 tell you? (Signal.) *Five parts in each whole.*
j. Make 5 parts in each whole for the first problem. ✔
k. Work the rest of the problems in Part 2 the same way. The bottom number tells how many parts to make in each whole. You have 4 minutes.
- (Observe students and give feedback.)

EXERCISE 3

Numerator Introduction

a. What does the bottom number of a fraction tell? (Signal.) *How many parts in each whole.*

b. (Write on the board:)

$$\frac{}{4}$$

- What does this number tell? (Signal.) *4 parts in each whole.*

c. (Write to show:)

$$\frac{1}{4}$$

- The top number tells how many parts are used. In this fraction, how many parts are used? (Signal.) *1.*

d. (Write on the board:)

$$\frac{6}{7}$$

- What does this bottom number tell? (Signal.) *7 parts in each whole.*
- In this fraction, how many parts are used? (Signal.) *6.*

e. (Repeat step d for: $\frac{8}{5}$ $\frac{3}{9}$ $\frac{5}{8}$.)

EXERCISE 4

Workcheck

a. We're going to check the answers. Exchange workbooks and get ready to check the answers. (Pause.)
Put an **X** next to each item that the person misses.

- (Check and correct.)
Part 1
Top row: 6, 6, 4, 7.
Next row: 8, 3, 2, 6.
Next row: 4, 7, 4, 8.
Last row: 3, 5, 6, 2.
Part 2
I'll tell you how many equal-sized parts there should be.
Top row: 5, 3, 2, 4.
Next row: 6, 2, 5, 3.
Next row: 4, 5, 2, 3.
Last row: 2, 6, 4, 3.
- Return the workbooks.

b. Now we're going to figure out the number of points you've earned for this lesson.
- (Point to the posted information.)

Worksheet Items	Errors	Points
	0–2	10
	3	7
	4	5
	5	3
	6	1
	7 or more	0

- Count the number of items you got wrong. Figure out the number of points you earned and write the number in the "Items" box.
- (Observe students and give feedback.)

c. (Tell the group how many points they earned for the lesson.) Write that number in the "Hard Work" box; then figure out the total for today's lesson.

d. Turn to the Point Summary Charts. Write the points in the box for Lesson 3. ✔

EXERCISE 1

Numerator Introduction

a. What does the bottom number of a fraction tell? (Signal.) *How many parts in each whole.*

b. (Write on the board:)

$$\frac{}{3}$$

- What does this number tell? (Signal.) *3 parts in each whole.*

c. (Write to show:)

$$\frac{2}{3}$$

- The top number tells how many parts are used. In this fraction, how many parts are used? (Signal.) *2.*

d. (Write on the board:)

$$\frac{5}{3}$$

- What does this bottom number tell? (Signal.) *3 parts in each whole.*
- In this fraction, how many parts are used? (Signal.) *5.*

e. (Repeat step d for: $\frac{7}{8}$ $\frac{6}{2}$ $\frac{2}{4}$.)

EXERCISE 2

Pictures to Fractions

a. (Draw on the board:)

★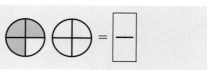

b. Look at this picture. We're going to write a fraction for this picture. Count to yourself. Figure out how many parts in each whole. (Pause.)

- How many parts in each whole? (Signal.) *4.*

c. Where do I write the 4? (Signal.) *On the bottom.*

d. (Write to show:)

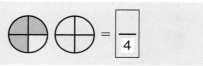

- Count to yourself. Figure out how many parts are used. Those are the ones that are shaded. (Pause.)
- How many parts are used? (Signal.) *3.*

e. Where do I write the 3? (Signal.) *On the top.*

f. (Write to show:)

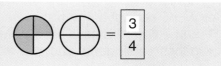

- This is a picture of 3 over 4.

Workbook Practice

a. Turn to Lesson 4 in your workbook. Touch the first problem in Part 1.

- Count to yourself. Figure out how many parts in each whole. (Pause.)
- How many parts in each whole? (Signal.) *3.*

b. Where do you write the 3? (Signal.) *On the bottom.*

c. Write the 3. ✔

d. Count to yourself. Figure out how many parts are used. Those are the shaded parts. (Pause.)
- How many parts are used? (Signal.) *4.*

e. Where do you write the 4? (Signal.) *On the top.*

f. Write the 4. ✔
- (Write on the board:)

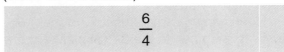

$$\frac{4}{3}$$

- Check your work. This is what you should have.

g. Touch the next problem.
- Count to yourself. Figure out how many parts in each whole. (Pause.)
- How many parts in each whole? (Signal.) *4.*

h. Write the 4. ✔

i. Count to yourself. Figure out how many parts are used. Those are the shaded parts. (Pause.)
- How many parts are used? (Signal.) *6.*

j. Write the 6. ✔
- (Write on the board:)

$$\frac{6}{4}$$

- Check your work. This is what you should have.

k. Work the rest of the problems in Part 1 the same way. You have 10 minutes.
- (Observe students and give feedback.)

EXERCISE 3

Workcheck

a. We're going to check the answers. Exchange workbooks and get ready to check the answers. (Pause.)
Put an **X** next to each item that the person misses.
- (Check and correct.)
Part 1
Top row: 4 over 3, 6 over 4, 2 over 2, 7 over 6
(Say as above for remaining fractions:)
Next row: 2/5, 1/3, 9/8, 1/2
Next row: 7/4, 3/7, 5/6, 6/3
Next row: 2/2, 11/8, 4/5, 3/2
Next row: 1/4, 3/5, 3/2, 8/6
Next row: 2/3, 4/3, 5/7, 3/8
Next row: 8/5, 2/2, 10/9, 2/6
Last row: 4/8, 3/7, 2/4, 3/3
- Return the workbooks.

b. Now we're going to figure out the number of points you've earned for this lesson.
- (Point to the posted information.)

Worksheet Items	Errors	Points
	0–2	10
	3	7
	4	5
	5	3
	6	1
	7 or more	0

- Count the number of items you got wrong. Figure out the number of points you earned and write the number in the "Items" box.
- (Observe students and give feedback.)

c. (Tell the group how many points they earned for the lesson.) Write that number in the "Hard Work" box; then figure out the total for today's lesson.

d. Turn to the Point Summary Charts. Write the points in the box for Lesson 4. ✔

Skipping Note: Check the students' errors from Lesson 4. If no more than 1 fourth of the students made more than 4 errors, do only the Fraction Naming exercise from this lesson. Then proceed with Lesson 6.

EXERCISE 1

Fraction Naming

a. We're going to learn the names of some fractions.
- (Write on the board:)

$$\frac{1}{4}$$

- (Touch the 1.) This fraction is 1 (touch the 4) fourth.
- Read this fraction. (Touch the 1 and then the 4 as the students read:) *1 fourth.*

b. (Change to show:)

$$\frac{5}{4}$$

- (Touch the 5.) This fraction is 5 (touch the 4) fourths.
- Read this fraction. (Touch the 5 and then the 4 as the students read:) *5 fourths.*

c. (Change to show:)

$$\frac{3}{4}$$

- (Touch the 3.) This fraction is 3 (touch the 4) fourths.
- Read this fraction. (Touch the 3 and then the 4 as the students read:) *3 fourths.*

d. (Change to show:)

$$\frac{6}{4}$$

- I won't touch this one. Just read it. (Signal.) *6 fourths.*

e. (Write on the board:)

$$\frac{5}{6}$$

- This fraction is 5 sixths.
- How do you read this fraction? (Signal.) *5 sixths.*

f. (Change to show:)

$$\frac{2}{6}$$

- How do you read this fraction? (Signal.) *2 sixths.*

g. (Change the 2 to a 7.)

$$\frac{7}{6}$$

- How do you read this fraction? (Signal.) *7 sixths.*

h. (Write on the board:)

$$\frac{3}{7}$$

- This fraction is 3 sevenths.
- How do you read this fraction? (Signal.) *3 sevenths.*

i. (Change the 3 to an 8.)
- How do you read this fraction? (Signal.) *8 sevenths.*

j. (Change the 8 to a 7.)
- How do you read this fraction? (Signal.) *7 sevenths.*

k. (Write on the board:)

★

$$\frac{2}{7} \quad \frac{3}{4} \quad \frac{1}{6} \quad \frac{8}{7} \quad \frac{5}{4} \quad \frac{1}{4} \quad \frac{4}{6} \quad \frac{7}{6} \quad \frac{5}{7}$$

- Read each fraction when I touch it. (Touch each fraction.)
- (Repeat any that are difficult.)

Lesson 5

EXERCISE 2

Numerator Introduction

a. What does the bottom number of a fraction tell? (Signal.) *How many parts in each whole.*

b. (Write on the board:)

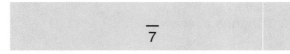

* What does this number tell? (Signal.) *7 parts in each whole.*

c. (Write to show:)

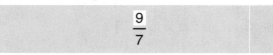

* The top number tells how many parts are used. In this fraction, how many parts are used? (Signal.) *9.*

d. (Write on the board:)

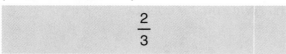

* What does this bottom number tell? (Signal.) *3 parts in each whole.*
* In this fraction, how many parts are used? (Signal.) *2.*

e. (Repeat step d for $\frac{5}{7}$ and $\frac{3}{9}$.)

EXERCISE 3

Pictures to Fractions

a. (Draw on the board:)

★
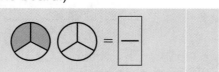

b. Look at this picture. We're going to write a fraction for this picture. Count to yourself. Figure out how many parts in each whole. (Pause.)

* How many parts in each whole? (Signal.) *3.*

c. Where do I write the 3? (Signal.) *On the bottom.*

d. (Write to show:)

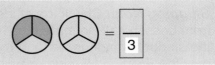

* Count to yourself. Figure out how many parts are used. The used parts are the ones that are shaded. (Pause.)
* How many parts are used? (Signal.) *2.*

e. Where do I write the 2? (Signal.) *On the top.*

f. (Write to show:)

* This is a picture of 2 over 3.

Workbook Practice

a. Turn to Lesson 5 in your workbook. Touch the first problem in Part 1.

* Count to yourself. Figure out how many parts in each whole. (Pause.)
* How many parts in each whole? (Signal.) *6.*

b. Where do you write the 6? (Signal.) *On the bottom.*

c. Write the 6. ✔

d. Count to yourself. Figure out how many parts are used. Those are the shaded parts. (Pause.)

* How many parts are used? (Signal.) *4.*

e. Where do you write the 4? (Signal.) *On the top.*

f. Write the 4. ✔

* (Write on the board:)

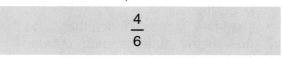

* Check your work. This is what you should have.

g. Look at the next problem.

* Count to yourself. Figure out how many parts in each whole. (Pause.)
* How many parts in each whole? (Signal.) *2.*

h. Write the 2. ✔
i. Count to yourself. Figure out how many parts are used. Those are the shaded parts. (Pause.)
• How many parts are used? (Signal.) *2.*
j. Write the 2. ✔
k. Work the rest of the problems in Part 1 the same way. You have 10 minutes.
• (Observe students and give feedback.)

EXERCISE 4

Workcheck

a. We're going to check the answers. Exchange workbooks and get ready to check the answers. (Pause.)
Put an **X** next to each item that the person misses.
• (Check and correct.)
Part 1
Top row: 4 over 6, 2 over 2, 2 over 3, 11 over 6
(Say as above for remaining fractions:)
Next row: 10/8, 1/5, 3/4, 6/7
Next row: 4/2, 1/3, 2/6, 9/7
Next row: 3/5, 2/4, 1/9, 5/8
Next row: 3/3, 1/2, 4/5, 8/6
Next row: 8/4, 1/7, 2/8, 1/2
Next row: 10/8, 1/4, 1/3, 10/7
Last row: 2/2, 2/5, 3/6, 8/8
• Return the workbooks.

b. Now we're going to figure out the number of points you've earned for this lesson.
• (Point to the posted information.)

Worksheet Items	Errors	Points
	0–2	10
	3	7
	4	5
	5	3
	6	1
	7 or more	0

• Count the number of items you got wrong. Figure out the number of points you earned and write the number in the "Items" box.
• (Observe students and give feedback.)
c. (Tell the group how many points they earned for the lesson.) Write that number in the "Hard Work" box; then figure out the total for today's lesson.
d. Turn to the Point Summary Charts. Write the points in the box for Lesson 5. ✔
e. Total your points for Lessons 1 through 5 and write the total number on the chart.
• (Observe students and give feedback.)
f. Everybody, find the Five-Lesson Point Graph on page 76. ✔
• (Help the students plot their five-lesson scores on the graph.)

EXERCISE 1

Fraction Naming

a. (Write on the board:)

$$\frac{5}{4}$$

- (Touch the 5.) This fraction is 5 (touch the 4) fourths.
- Read this fraction. *5 fourths.*

b. (Change the 5 to a 3.)
- (Touch the 3.) This fraction is 3 (touch the 4) fourths.
- Read this fraction. *3 fourths.*

c. (Change the 3 to a 6.)
- Read this fraction. *6 fourths.*

d. (Write on the board:)

$$\frac{3}{7}$$

- This fraction is 3 sevenths.
- How do you read this fraction? (Signal.) *3 sevenths.*

e. (Change the 3 to an 8.)
- How do you read this fraction? (Signal.) *8 sevenths.*

f. (Write on the board:)

$$\frac{1}{6}$$

- This fraction is 1 sixth.
- How do you read this fraction? (Signal.) *1 sixth.*

g. (Change the 1 to a 7.)
- How do you read this fraction? (Signal.) *7 sixths.*

h. (Write on the board:)
★

$$\frac{6}{4} \quad \frac{3}{6} \quad \frac{5}{7} \quad \frac{9}{7} \quad \frac{2}{4} \quad \frac{7}{6}$$

- Read each fraction when I touch it. (Touch each fraction.)
- (Repeat any that are difficult.)

EXERCISE 2

Pictures to Fractions

a. Turn to Lesson 6 in your workbook. Touch the first problem in Part 1.
- You have to write the fraction for that picture. Count to yourself. Figure out how many parts in each whole. (Pause.)
- How many parts in each whole? (Signal.) *5.*

b. Where do you write the 5? (Signal.) *On the bottom.*
- Write the 5. ✔

c. Count to yourself. Figure out how many parts are used. Those are the shaded parts. (Pause.)
- How many parts are used? (Signal.) *3.*

d. Where do you write the 3? (Signal.) *On the top.*
- Write the 3. ✔

e. Look at the next problem.
- Count to yourself. Figure out how many parts in each whole. (Pause.)
- How many parts in each whole? (Signal.) *3.*
- Write the 3. ✔

f. Count to yourself. Figure out how many parts are used. (Pause.)
- How many parts are used? (Signal.) *5.*
- Write the 5. ✔

g. Work the rest of the problems in Part 1 the same way. You have 5 minutes.
- (Observe students and give feedback.)

Lesson 6

EXERCISE 3

Fractions to Pictures

a. (Draw on the board:)

★

b. We have to make a picture for this fraction. What does this bottom number tell us? (Signal.) *3 parts in each whole.*

c. We have to make 3 parts in each whole.
- (Divide each circle into 3 equal parts.)
- There are 3 parts in each whole.

d. (Touch $\frac{2}{3}$.)
- In this fraction, how many parts are used? (Signal.) *2.*

e. I'll shade the parts that are used. How many parts do I shade? (Signal.) *2.*

f. (Shade 2 parts.)
- This is the picture for the fraction 2 over 3.

Workbook Practice

a. Touch the first problem in Part 2.
- You have to draw the picture for that fraction.
- What does the bottom number of that fraction tell? (Signal.) *4 parts in each whole.*

b. You have to make 4 parts in each whole. The first whole already has 4 parts. Make 4 parts in the next whole. ✔

c. Touch the first fraction. In that fraction, how many parts are used? (Signal.) *3.*
- So how many parts will you shade? (Signal.) *3.*
- Do it. ✔

d. Touch the next fraction in that row.
- What does the bottom number of that fraction tell? (Signal.) *2 parts in each whole.*
- You have to make 2 parts in each whole. Do it. ✔

e. In that fraction, how many parts are used? (Signal.) *1.*
- So how many parts will you shade? (Signal.) *1.*
- Do it. ✔

f. Work the rest of the problems in Part 2. Make the picture for each fraction. You have 5 minutes.
- (Observe students and give feedback.)

EXERCISE 4

Workcheck

a. We're going to check the answers. Exchange workbooks, and get ready to check the answers. (Pause.)
- Put an **X** next to each problem that the person misses.
- (Check and correct.)

Part 1
Top row: 3 over 5, 5 over 3, 8 over 8, 5 over 6
(Say as above for remaining fractions:)
Next row: 3/4, 7/7, 3/2, 3/8
Next row: 2/3, 4/4, 5/6, 2/8
Next row: 1/4, 6/5, 1/2, 6/7

Part 2
Top row:
4 parts in each whole, 3 parts shaded
2 parts in each whole, 1 part shaded
5 parts in each whole, 4 parts shaded
3 parts in each whole, 4 parts shaded
Next row:
2 parts in each whole, 3 parts shaded
4 parts in each whole, 1 part shaded
3 parts in each whole, 3 parts shaded
5 parts in each whole, 2 parts shaded
Next row:
4 parts in each whole, 6 parts shaded
3 parts in each whole, 1 part shaded
5 parts in each whole, 7 parts shaded
2 parts in each whole, 4 parts shaded
Last row:
5 parts in each whole, 4 parts shaded
3 parts in each whole, 5 parts shaded
2 parts in each whole, 2 parts shaded
4 parts in each whole, 4 parts shaded
- Return the workbooks.

b. Now we're going to figure out the number of points you've earned for this lesson.
- (Point to the posted information.)

Worksheet Items	Errors	Points
	0–2	10
	3	7
	4	5
	5	3
	6	1
	7 or more	0

- Count the number of items you got wrong. Figure out the number of points you earned and write the number in the "Items" box.
- (Observe students and give feedback.)

c. (Tell the group how many points they earned for the lesson.) Write that number in the "Hard Work" box; then figure out the total for today's lesson.

d. Turn to the Point Summary Charts. Write the points in the box for Lesson 6. ✔

Skipping Note: Check the students' errors from Lesson 6. If no more than 1 fourth of the students made more than 4 errors, do only the Fraction Naming exercise from this lesson. Then proceed with Lesson 8.

EXERCISE 1

Fraction Naming

a. (Write on the board:)

★
$$\frac{3}{4} \quad \frac{5}{7} \quad \frac{8}{6} \quad \frac{2}{7} \quad \frac{1}{6} \quad \frac{7}{4}$$

b. Let's go over the names of the fractions that we learned.
- Read each fraction when I touch it. (Touch each fraction.)
- (Repeat any that are difficult.)

c. We're going to learn the names of some other fractions.
- (Write on the board:)

$$\frac{3}{8}$$

- (Touch the 3.) This fraction is 3 (touch the 8) eighths.
- Read this fraction. (Touch the 3 and then the 8 as the students read:) *3 eighths.*

d. (Change the 3 to a 9. Touch the 9.)
- This fraction is 9 (touch the 8) eighths.
- Read this fraction. (Touch the 9 and then the 8 as the students read:) *9 eighths.*

e. (Change the 9 to a 6.)
- Read this fraction. (Touch the 6 and then the 8 as the students read:) *6 eighths.*

f. (Change the 6 to a 1.)
- I won't touch this one. Just read it. (Signal.) *1 eighth.*

g. (Write on the board:)

$$\frac{4}{9}$$

- This fraction is 4 ninths.
- How do you read this fraction? (Signal.) *4 ninths.*

h. (Change the 4 to a 12.)
- How do you read this fraction? (Signal.) *12 ninths.*

i. (Change the 12 to a 6.)
- How do you read this fraction? (Signal.) *6 ninths.*

j. (Write on the board:)

$$\frac{11}{10}$$

- This fraction is read 11 tenths.
- How do you read this fraction? (Signal.) *11 tenths.*

k. (Change the 11 to a 5.)
- How do you read this fraction? (Signal.) *5 tenths.*

l. (Change the 5 to a 9.)
- How do you read this fraction? (Signal.) *9 tenths.*

m. (Write on the board:)

★
$$\frac{3}{8} \quad \frac{4}{9} \quad \frac{7}{10} \quad \frac{11}{8} \quad \frac{12}{10} \quad \frac{10}{9} \quad \frac{5}{4} \quad \frac{6}{7}$$

- Read each fraction when I touch it. (Touch each fraction.)
- (Repeat any that are difficult.)

EXERCISE 2

Pictures to Fractions

a. Turn to Lesson 7 in your workbook. Touch the first problem in Part 1.
- Count to yourself. Figure out how many parts in each whole. (Pause.)
- How many parts are in each whole? (Signal.) *4.*

b. Where do you write the 4? (Signal.) *On the bottom.*
- Write the 4. ✔

c. Count to yourself. Figure out how many parts are used. Those are the shaded parts. (Pause.)
• How many parts are used? (Signal.) *6.*
d. Where do you write the 6? (Signal.) *On the top.*
• Write the 6. ✔
e. Touch the next problem.
• Count to yourself. Figure out how many parts are in each whole. (Pause.)
• How many parts in each whole? (Signal.) *5.*
f. Write the 5. ✔
g. Count to yourself. Figure out how many parts are used. Those are the shaded parts. (Pause.)
• How many parts are used? (Signal.) *4.*
• Write the 4. ✔
h. Work the rest of the problems in Part 1 the same way. You have 5 minutes.
• (Observe students and give feedback.)

EXERCISE 3

Fractions to Pictures

a. (Draw on the board:)
★
b. We have to make a picture for this fraction. What does the bottom number tell us? (Signal.) *2 parts in each whole.*
c. We have to make 2 parts in each whole.
• (Divide each circle into 2 parts.)
• There are 2 parts in each whole.
d. (Touch $\frac{3}{2}$.)
• In this fraction, how many parts are used? (Signal.) *3.*
e. So how many parts do I shade? (Signal.) *3.*
f. (Shade 3 parts.)
• This is the picture for the fraction 3 over 2.

Workbook Practice

a. Touch the first problem in Part 2.
• You have to draw the picture for that fraction.
• What does the bottom number of that fraction tell? (Signal.) *3 parts in each whole.*
b. You have to make 3 parts in each whole. The first whole already has 3 parts. Make 3 parts in the next whole. ✔
c. In that first fraction, how many parts are used? (Signal.) *2.*
• So how many parts will you shade? (Signal.) *2.*
• Do it. ✔
d. Work the rest of the problems in Part 2. Make the picture for each fraction. You have 5 minutes.
• (Observe students and give feedback.)

EXERCISE 4

Workcheck

a. We're going to check the answers. Exchange workbooks, and get ready to check the answers. (Pause.)
• Put an X next to each problem that the person misses.
• (Check and correct.)
Part 1
Top row: 6 over 4, 4 over 5, 3 over 3, 3 over 7
(Say as above for remaining fractions:)
Next row: 9/6, 2/2, 2/5, 7/8
Next row: 2/4, 4/3, 3/8, 6/5
Next row: 3/2, 8/6, 5/7, 1/3
Part 2
Top row:
3 parts in each whole, 2 parts shaded
2 parts in each whole, 1 part shaded
4 parts in each whole, 4 parts shaded
5 parts in each whole, 2 parts shaded
Next row:
5 parts in each whole, 1 part shaded.
3 parts in each whole, 6 parts shaded
4 parts in each whole, 1 part shaded
2 parts in each whole, 3 parts shaded

Next row:
4 parts in each whole, 6 parts shaded
4 parts in each whole, 5 parts shaded
2 parts in each whole, 2 parts shaded
3 parts in each whole, 4 parts shaded
Last row:
5 parts in each whole, 7 parts shaded
2 parts in each whole, 4 parts shaded
4 parts in each whole, 3 parts shaded
3 parts in each whole, 1 part shaded

- Return the workbooks.

b. Now we're going to figure out the number of points you've earned for this lesson.

- (Point to the posted information.)

Worksheet Items	Errors	Points
	0–2	10
	3	7
	4	5
	5	3
	6	1
	7 or more	0

- Count the number of items you got wrong. Figure out the number of points you earned and write the number in the "Items" box.
- (Observe students and give feedback.)

c. (Tell the group how many points they earned for the lesson.) Write that number in the "Hard Work" box; then figure out the total for today's lesson.

d. Turn to the Point Summary Charts. Write the points in the box for Lesson 7. ✔

Lesson 8

EXERCISE 1

Fraction Naming

a. (Write on the board:)

★

$$\frac{3}{4} \quad \frac{2}{10} \quad \frac{1}{8} \quad \frac{9}{7} \quad \frac{10}{6} \quad \frac{7}{8}$$

b. Let's go over the names of the fractions that we learned.
- Read each fraction when I touch it. (Touch each fraction.)
- (Repeat any that are difficult.)

EXERCISE 2

Fractions to Pictures

a. Turn to Lesson 8 in your workbook. Touch the first problem in Part 1.
- You have to draw the picture for that fraction.
- What does the bottom number of that fraction tell? (Signal.) *2 parts in each whole.*
b. You have to make 2 parts in each whole. Make 2 parts in each whole. ✔
c. In that fraction, how many parts are used? (Signal.) *4.*
- So how many parts will you shade? (Signal.) *4.*
- Do it. ✔
d. Work the rest of the problems in Part 1. Make the picture for each fraction. You have 3 minutes.
- (Observe students and give feedback.)

EXERCISE 3

Pictures to Fractions

a. Touch the first problem in Part 2.
- Count to yourself. Figure out how many parts in each whole. (Pause.)
- How many parts in each whole? (Signal.) *6.*
- Write the 6. ✔
b. Count to yourself. Figure out how many parts are used. (Pause.)
- How many parts are used? (Signal.) *5.*
- Write the 5. ✔
c. Touch the next problem in Part 2.
- Count to yourself. Figure out how many parts in each whole. (Pause.)
- How many parts in each whole? (Signal.) *3.*
- Write the 3. ✔
d. Count to yourself. Figure out how many parts are used. (Pause.)
- How many parts are used? (Signal.) *6.*
- Write the 6. ✔
e. Work the rest of the problems in Part 2 the same way. You have 3 minutes.
- (Observe students and give feedback.)

EXERCISE 4

Equals 1—With Pictures

a. (Draw on the board:)

★

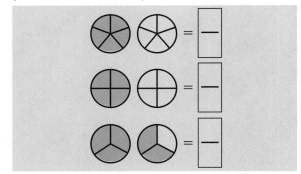

b. Here's a rule about fractions that equal 1. A fraction equals 1 when you use the same number of parts that are in each whole. Listen again. A fraction equals 1 when you use the same number of parts that are in each whole.

c. (Touch the first row of fraction pictures.)

- Look at this picture. Tell me, how many parts are in each whole? (Pause.) Get ready. (Signal.) *5.*
- (Write to show:)

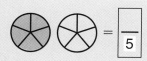

d. Tell me how many parts are used. (Pause.) Get ready. (Signal.) *5.*
- (Write to show:)

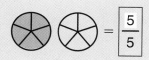

- You use the same number of parts that are in each whole. The fraction equals 1 whole.
- (Write to show:)

New Problem

a. (Touch the second row of fraction pictures.)

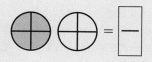

- In this fraction, tell me how many parts are in each whole. (Pause.) Get ready. (Signal.) *4.*
b. (Write to show:)

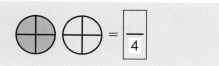

c. Tell me how many parts are used. (Pause.) Get ready. (Signal.) *4.*
- (Write to show:)

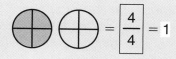

- Do you use the same number of parts that are in each whole? (Signal.) *Yes.*
- So the fraction equals 1.
- (Write to show:)

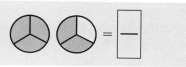

New Problem

a. (Touch the third row of fraction pictures.)

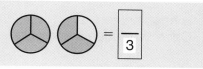

- In this picture, how many parts are in each whole? (Pause.) Get ready. (Signal.) *3.*
b. (Write to show:)

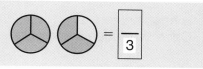

c. How many parts are used? (Pause.) Get ready. (Signal.) *5.*
- (Write to show:)

· Do you use the same number of parts that are in each whole? (Signal.) *No.*
- This fraction does not equal 1.

Workbook Practice

a. Look at Part 3 in your workbook.
- The first problem is already worked. There are 5 parts in each whole. How many parts are used? (Signal.) *5.*

- Do you use the same number of parts that are in each whole? (Signal.) *Yes.*
- So the fraction equals 1. It equals 1 whole. That's what's written. **Equals 1.**

b. Touch the next problem.
- Write the fraction for the picture. ✔

c. Now we'll see whether the fraction equals 1. Remember, a fraction equals 1 when you use the same number of parts that are in each whole.
- In this picture, how many parts are in each whole? (Signal.) *7.*
- Do you use the same number of parts that are in each whole? (Signal.) *Yes.*
- So does that fraction equal 1? (Signal.) *Yes.*
- Write **equals 1** after that fraction. ✔

d. Now write the fraction for the next picture. ✔
- How many parts are in each whole? (Signal.) *7.*
- Do you use the same number of parts that are in each whole? (Signal.) *No.*
- So does that fraction equal 1? (Signal.) *No.*
- Don't write **equals 1** for that fraction. ✔

e. Work the rest of the problems in Part 3. First write the fraction for the picture. Then figure out whether the fraction equals 1. If the fraction equals 1, write **equals 1.** You have 4 minutes.
- (Observe students and give feedback.)

EXERCISE 5

Workcheck

a. We're going to check the answers. Exchange workbooks, and get ready to check the answers. (Pause.)
- Put an **X** next to each problem that the person misses.
- (Check and correct.)
  Part 1
  Top row:
  2 parts in each whole, 4 parts shaded
  5 parts in each whole, 3 parts shaded
  3 parts in each whole, 2 parts shaded
  4 parts in each whole, 5 parts shaded

Next row:
5 parts in each whole, 7 parts shaded
2 parts in each whole, 1 part shaded
4 parts in each whole, 3 parts shaded
3 parts in each whole, 3 parts shaded
Last row:
3 parts in each whole, 5 parts shaded
5 parts in each whole, 4 parts shaded
2 parts in each whole, 3 parts shaded
4 parts in each whole, 2 parts shaded
Part 2
Top row: 5 over 6, 6 over 3, 5 over 4, 4 over 5
(Say as above for remaining fractions:)
Next row: 11/8, 4/7, 1/2, 8/6
Part 3
Top row: 5/5 equals 1; 7/7 equals 1; 9/7
Next row: 6/6 = 1; 3/3 = 1; 3/4
Last row: 3/2; 5/5 = 1; 3/3 = 1

- Return the workbooks.

b. Now we're going to figure out the number of points you've earned for this lesson.
- (Point to the posted information.)

Worksheet Items	Errors	Points
	0–2	10
	3	7
	4	5
	5	3
	6	1
	7 or more	0

- Count the number of items you got wrong. Figure out the number of points you earned and write the number in the "Items" box.
- (Observe students and give feedback.)

c. (Tell the group how many points they earned for the lesson.) Write that number in the "Hard Work" box; then figure out the total for today's lesson.

d. Turn to the Point Summary Charts. Write the points in the box for Lesson 8. ✔

EXERCISE 1

Fraction Naming

a. (Write on the board:)

★

$$\frac{6}{7} \quad \frac{5}{4} \quad \frac{3}{6} \quad \frac{2}{9} \quad \frac{7}{10} \quad \frac{9}{8}$$

- Let's go over the names of the fractions that we learned.
- Read each fraction when I touch it. (Touch each fraction.)
- (Repeat any that are difficult.)

b. We're going to learn the names of some other fractions.
- (Write on the board:)

$$\frac{2}{5}$$

- (Touch the 2.) This fraction is 2 (touch the 5) fifths.
- Read this fraction. (Touch the 2 and then the 5 as the students read:) *2 fifths.*

c. (Change the 2 to a 7.)
- (Touch the 7.) This fraction is 7 (touch the 5) fifths.
- Read this fraction. (Touch the 7 and then the 5 as the students read:) *7 fifths.*

d. (Change the 7 to a 4.)
- Read this fraction. (Touch the 4 and then the 5 as the students read:) *4 fifths.*

e. (Change the 4 to a 1.)
- I won't touch this one. Just read it. (Signal.) *1 fifth.*

f. (Write on the board:)

$$\frac{2}{3}$$

- This fraction is 2 thirds.
- How do you read this fraction? (Signal.) *2 thirds.*

g. (Change the 2 to a 6.)
- How do you read this fraction? (Signal.) *6 thirds.*

h. (Change the 6 to a 1.)
- How do you read this fraction? (Signal.) *1 third.*

i. (Write on the board:)

$$\frac{2}{3} \quad \frac{4}{5} \quad \frac{1}{5} \quad \frac{5}{3} \quad \frac{1}{6} \quad \frac{3}{4} \quad \frac{1}{3} \quad \frac{2}{7} \quad \frac{1}{5}$$

- Read each fraction when I touch it. (Touch each fraction.)
- (Repeat any that are difficult.)

EXERCISE 2

Pictures to Fractions

a. Turn to Lesson 9 in your workbook. Touch the first problem in Part 1.
- First count to yourself how many parts in each whole. (Pause.)
- How many parts in each whole? (Signal.) *4.*
- Write the 4. ✔

b. Count to yourself how many parts are used. (Pause.)
- How many parts are used? (Signal.) *3.*
- Write the 3. ✔

c. Work the rest of the problems in Part 1 the same way. You have 3 minutes.
- (Observe students and give feedback.)

EXERCISE 3

Equals 1—With Pictures

a. Remember the rule about fractions that equal 1. A fraction equals 1 when you use the same number of parts that are in each whole.

b. Look at Part 2 in your workbook.
- The first problem is already worked. There are 3 parts in each whole. How many parts are used? (Signal.) *3.*
- Do you use the same number of parts that are in each whole? (Signal.) *Yes.*
- So the fraction equals 1. It equals 1 whole. That's what's written. **Equals 1.**

c. Touch the next problem.
- Write the fraction for the picture. ✔

d. Now we'll see whether the fraction equals 1. Remember, a fraction equals 1 when you use the same number of parts that are in each whole.

- In this fraction, how many parts are in each whole? (Signal.) *4.*
- How many parts do you use? (Signal.) *4.*
- Do you use the same number of parts that are in each whole? (Signal.) *Yes.*
- So does that fraction equal 1? (Signal.) *Yes.*
- Write **equals 1** after that fraction. ✔
e. Now write the fraction for the next picture. ✔
- How many parts are in each whole? (Signal.) *6.*
- How many parts do you use? (Signal.) *3.*
- Do you use the same number of parts that are in each whole? (Signal.) *No.*
- So does that fraction equal 1? (Signal.) *No.*
- Don't write **equals 1** after that fraction. ✔
f. Work the rest of the problems in Part 2. First write the fraction for the picture. Then figure out whether it equals 1. If the fraction equals 1, write **equals 1.** You have 6 minutes.
- (Observe students and give feedback.)

EXERCISE 4

Workcheck

a. We're going to check the answers. Exchange workbooks, and get ready to check the answers. (Pause.)
- Put an **X** next to each problem that the person misses.

- (Check and correct.)
Part 1
Top row: 3 over 4, 13 over 7, 7 over 6, 4 over 5
(Say as above for remaining fractions:)
Next row: 5/3, 7/5, 2/6, 3/2
Last row: 7/4, 1/2, 5/8, 8/7
Part 2
Top row: 3/3 equals 1; 4/4 equals 1; 3/6
Next row: 2/2 = 1; 4/5; 8/8 = 1
Next row: 10/7; 4/3; 5/5 = 1
Next row: 4/3; 6/6 = 1; 8/5
Last row: 6/4; 8/5; 6/9
- Return the workbooks.
b. Now we're going to figure out the number of points you've earned for this lesson.
- (Point to the posted information.)

Worksheet Items	Errors	Points
	0–2	10
	3	7
	4	5
	5	3
	6	1
	7 or more	0

- Count the number of items you got wrong. Figure out the number of points you earned and write the number in the "Items" box.
- (Observe students and give feedback.)
c. (Tell the group how many points they earned for the lesson.) Write that number in the "Hard Work" box; then figure out the total for today's lesson.
d. Turn to the Point Summary Charts. Write the points in the box for Lesson 9. ✔

Lesson 10

EXERCISE 1

Fractions to Pictures

a. Turn to Lesson 10 in your workbook. Touch the first problem in Part 1.
- You have to draw the picture for that fraction.
- What does the bottom number of that fraction tell? (Signal.) *3 parts in each whole.*

b. Make 3 parts in each whole. ✔

c. In that fraction, how many parts will you shade? (Signal.) *2.*
- Do it. ✔

d. Work the rest of the problems in Part 1. Make the picture for each fraction. You have 3 minutes.

EXERCISE 2

Equals 1

a. Look at Part 2 in your workbook.
- Write the fraction for the picture. ✔

b. Now we'll see whether the fraction equals 1. Remember, a fraction equals 1 when you use the same number of parts that are in each whole.
- In this fraction, how many parts are in each whole? (Signal.) *6.*
- How many parts do you use? (Signal.) *6.*
- Do you use the same number of parts that are in each whole? (Signal.) *Yes.*
- So does that fraction equal 1? (Signal.) *Yes.*
- Write **equals 1** after that fraction. ✔

c. Now write the fraction for the next picture. ✔
- How many parts are in each whole? (Signal.) *4.*
- How many parts do you use? (Signal.) *5.*
- Do you use the same number of parts that are in each whole? (Signal.) *No.*
- So does that fraction equal 1? (Signal.) *No.*
- Don't write **equals 1** after that fraction.

d. Work the rest of the problems in Part 2. First write the fraction for the picture. Then figure out whether the fraction equals 1. If the fraction equals 1, write equals 1. You have 3 minutes.
- (Observe students and give feedback.)

EXERCISE 3

Equals 1—No Pictures

a. (Write on the board:)

$$\frac{9}{9}$$

- How many parts in each whole? (Signal.) *9.*
- How any parts are used? (Signal.) *9.*
- Does this fraction equal 1? (Signal.) *Yes.*

b. Here's how we know the fraction equals 1: because you use the same number of parts that are in each whole.
- Your turn. How do you know this fraction equals 1? (Signal.) *You use the same number of parts that are in each whole.*
- (Repeat until firm.)

c. (Write on the board:)

$$\frac{5}{9}$$

- Does this fraction equal 1? (Signal.) *No.*

d. Here's how we know the fraction doesn't equal 1: because you don't use the same number of parts that are in each whole.
- Your turn. How do you know that this fraction doesn't equal 1? (Signal.) *You don't use the same number of parts that are in each whole.*
- (Repeat until firm.)

e. Touch the first problem in Part 3.
- Does that fraction equal 1? (Signal.) *Yes.*
- How do you know? (Signal.) *You use the same number of parts that are in each whole.*
- Write **equals 1** after that fraction. ✔

f. Touch the next problem. ✔
- Does this fraction equal 1? (Signal.) *No.*
- How do you know? (Signal.) *You don't use the same number of parts that are in each whole.*
- Don't write **equals 1** after that fraction.

g. Work the rest of the problems in Part 3. If the fraction equals 1, write **equals 1.** You have 4 minutes.
- (Observe students and give feedback.)

Lesson 10

EXERCISE 4

Fraction Naming

a. (Write on the board:)

★

$$\frac{2}{5} \quad \frac{1}{3} \quad \frac{2}{7} \quad \frac{4}{7} \quad \frac{3}{8} \quad \frac{7}{9} \quad \frac{5}{10} \quad \frac{5}{6} \quad \frac{7}{4}$$

- Let's go over the names of the fractions that we learned.
- Read each fraction when I touch it. (Touch each fraction.)
- (Repeat any that are difficult.)

EXERCISE 5

Workcheck

a. We're going to check the answers. Exchange workbooks, and get ready to check the answers. (Pause.)
- Put an **X** next to each problem that the person misses.
- (Check and correct.)
  Part 1
  Top row:
  3 parts in each whole, 2 parts shaded
  5 parts in each whole, 7 parts shaded
  4 parts in each whole, 5 parts shaded
  2 parts in each whole, 3 parts shaded
  Next row:
  4 parts in each whole, 3 parts shaded
  5 parts in each whole, 2 parts shaded
  3 parts in each whole, 3 parts shaded
  2 parts in each whole, 1 part shaded
  Part 2
  Top row: 6/6 equals 1; 5/4; 3/2
  Next row: 4/3; 5/5 = 1; 8/8 = 1

Part 3
Top row: 4/4 equals 1; 7/4; 3/5; 9/9 equals 1; 7/7 equals 1; 9/6
Next row: 3/4, 3/3 =1; 8/8 = 1; 5/4; 2/2 = 1; 1/5
Next row: 5/5 = 1; 7/3; 6/6 = 1; 4/4 = 1; 4/3; 6/7
Last row: 10/10 = 1; 5/6; 7/6; 6/9; 8/8 = 1; 4/4 = 1

- Return the workbooks.
b. Now we're going to figure out the number of points you've earned for this lesson.
- (Point to the posted information.)

Worksheet Items	Errors	Points
	0–2	10
	3	7
	4	5
	5	3
	6	1
	7 or more	0

- Count the number of items you got wrong. Figure out the number of points you earned and write the number in the "Item" box.
- (Observe students and give feedback.)
c. (Tell the group how many points they earned for the lesson.) Write that number in the "Hard Work" box; then figure out the total for today's lesson.
d. Turn to the Point Summary Charts. Write the points in the box for Lesson 10. ✔
e. Total your points for Lessons 6 through 10 and write the total number on the chart.
- (Observe students and give feedback.)
f. Everybody, find the Five-Lesson Point Graph on page 76. ✔
- (Help the students plot their five-lesson scores on the graph.)

26 Lesson 10

EXERCISE 1

Fraction Naming

a. (*Before the lesson, write on the board:)

★

$$\frac{2}{4} \quad \frac{8}{7} \quad \frac{4}{5} \quad \frac{2}{3} \quad \frac{1}{6} \quad \frac{10}{9} \quad \frac{2}{7}$$

$$\frac{5}{8} \quad \frac{6}{10} \quad \frac{8}{5} \quad \frac{6}{3} \quad \frac{3}{2} \quad \frac{4}{5} \quad \frac{1}{3}$$

$$\frac{7}{6} \quad \frac{5}{2} \quad \frac{1}{2} \quad \frac{8}{5} \quad \frac{2}{7} \quad \frac{5}{3} \quad \frac{4}{2}$$

- Let's go over the names of the fractions that we learned.
- Read each fraction when I touch it. (Touch each fraction.)
- (Repeat any that are difficult.)

b. (Write on the board:)

$$\frac{1}{2}$$

- This fraction is funny. This fraction is read **1 half.**
- How do you read this fraction? (Signal.) *1 half.*

c. (Change the 1 to a 3. Touch the 3.)
- This fraction is 3 (touch the 2) halves.
- Read this fraction. (Touch the 3 and then the 2 as the students read:) *3 halves.*

d. (Change the 3 to a 5. Touch the 5.)
- Read this fraction. (Signal.) *5 halves.*

e. (Change the 5 to a 1.)
- Just read it. (Signal.) *1 half.*

f. (Point to the second row of fractions you wrote on the board.)
- Read each fraction when I touch it. (Touch each fraction.)
- (Repeat any that are difficult.)

EXERCISE 2

Fractions to Pictures

a. Turn to Lesson 11 in your workbook. Touch the first problem in Part 1.
- You have to draw the picture for that fraction.
- What does the bottom number of that fraction tell? (Signal.) *6 parts in each whole.*

b. Make 6 parts in each whole. ✔

c. In that fraction, how many parts will you shade? (Signal.) 5
- Do it. ✔

d. Work the rest of the problems in Part 1. Make the picture for each fraction. You have 3 minutes.
- (Observe students and give feedback.)

EXERCISE 3

Equals 1

a. (Write on the board:)

$$\frac{5}{5}$$

- How many parts in each whole? (Signal.) *5.*
- How any parts are used? (Signal.) *5.*

b. Does that fraction equal 1? (Signal.) *Yes.*
- Here's how we know the fraction equals 1. Because we use the same number of parts that are in each whole.
- Your turn. How do you know this fraction equals 1? (Signal.) *You use the same number of parts that are in each whole.*
- (Repeat until firm.)

c. (Write on the board:)

$$\frac{4}{5}$$

- Does that fraction equal 1? (Signal.) *No.*
- Here's how we know it doesn't equal 1. Because we don't use the same number of parts that are in each whole.

- Your turn. How do you know that this fraction doesn't equal 1? (Signal.) *You don't use the same number of parts that are in each whole.*
- (Repeat until firm.)

d. Touch the first problem in Part 2.
- Read that fraction. (Signal.) *7 sevenths.*
- Does that fraction equal 1? (Signal.) *Yes.*
- How do you know? (Signal.) *You use the same number of parts that are in each whole.*
- Write **equals 1** after that fraction. ✔

e. Touch the next problem.
- Does that fraction equal 1? (Signal.) *No.*
- How do you know? (Signal.) *You don't use the same number of parts that are in each whole.*
- Don't write **equals 1** after that fraction.

f. Work the rest of the problems in Part 2. If the fraction equals 1, write equals 1. You have 2 minutes.
- (Observe students and give feedback.)

EXERCISE 4

More, Less, Equal to 1

a. A fraction equals 1 when you use the same number of parts that are in each whole.
- A fraction is more than 1 when you use more parts than are in each whole.
- A fraction is less than 1 when you use less parts than are in each whole.

b. (Write on the board:)

★

$$\frac{7}{4} \genfrac{}{}{0pt}{}{\text{more}}{=}_{\text{less}}$$

- Does this fraction equal 1? (Signal.) *No.*
- How do you know? (Signal.) *You don't use the same number of parts that are in each whole.*
- (Repeat until firm.)

c. In this fraction, how many parts are in each whole? (Signal.) *4.*
- Do you use more than 4 parts or less than 4 parts? (Signal.) *More.*

- So the fraction is more than 1. I'll circle the word **more.**
- (Circle **more.**)

d. Touch the first problem in Part 3.
- Does that fraction equal 1? (Signal.) *No.*
- How do you know? (Signal.) *You don't use the same number of parts that are in each whole.*
- How many parts are in each whole? (Signal.) *7.*
- Do you use more than 7 parts or less than 7 parts? (Signal.) *Less.*
- So is that fraction more than 1 or less than 1? (Signal.) *Less.*
- Circle the word **less.**

e. Touch the next problem.
- Does that fraction equal 1? (Signal.) *Yes.*
- How do you know? (Signal.) *You use the same number of parts that are in each whole.*
- That fraction equals 1, so circle the **equals** sign. ✔

f. Touch the next problem.
- Does that fraction equal 1? (Signal.) *No.*
- How do you know? (Signal.) *You don't use the same number of parts that are in each whole.*
- How many parts are in each whole? (Signal.) *5.*
- Do you use more than 5 parts or less than 5 parts? (Signal.) *More.*
- So is that fraction more or less than 1? (Signal.) *More.*
- Circle the word **more.** ✔

g. Work the rest of the problems in Part 3 the same way. You have 5 minutes.
- (Observe students and give feedback.)

EXERCISE 5

Workcheck

a. We're going to check the answers. Exchange workbooks, and get ready to check the answers. (Pause.)
- Put an **X** next to each item that the person misses.
- (Check and correct. See **Answer Key.**)
- Return the workbooks.

b. Now we're going to figure out the number of points you've earned for this lesson.

- (Point to the posted information.)

Worksheet Items	Errors	Points
	0–2	10
	3	7
	4	5
	5	3
	6	1
	7 or more	0

- Count the number of items you got wrong. Figure out the number of points you earned and write the number in the "Items" box.
- (Observe students and give feedback.)

c. (Tell the group how many points they earned for the lesson.) Write that number in the "Hard Work" box; then figure out the total for today's lesson.

d. Turn to the Point Summary Charts. Write the points in the box for Lesson 11. ✔

Lesson 12

EXERCISE 1
Equals 1

a. (Write on the board:)

$$\frac{7}{7}$$

- In this fraction, how many parts are in each whole? (Signal.) *7.*
b. Does this fraction equal 1? (Signal.) *Yes.*
- We know because we use the same number of parts that are in each whole.
- Your turn. How do you know this fraction equals 1? (Signal.) *You use the same number of parts that are in each whole.*
- (Repeat until firm.)
c. (Write on the board:)

$$\frac{8}{7}$$

d. Does this fraction equal 1? (Signal.) *No.*
- We know because we don't use the same number of parts that are in each whole.
- Your turn. How do you know this fraction doesn't equal 1? (Signal.) *You don't use the same number of parts that are in each whole.*
- (Repeat until firm.)
e. Turn to Lesson 12 in your workbook. Touch the first problem in Part 1.
- Does that fraction equal 1? (Signal.) *Yes.*
- How do you know? (Signal.) *You use the same number of parts that are in each whole.*
- Write **equals 1** after that fraction. ✔
f. Touch the next problem.
- Does that fraction equal 1? (Signal.) *No.*
- How do you know? (Signal.) *You don't use the same number of parts that are in each whole.*
- Don't write **equals 1** after that fraction.
g. Work the rest of the problems in Part 1. If the fraction equals 1, write equals 1. You have 2 minutes.
- (Observe students and give feedback.)

EXERCISE 2
Making Fractions Equal 1

a. Touch the first problem in Part 2.
- All the fractions in this part equal 1, but part of each fraction is missing. You have to fill in the missing part. What does the bottom number of the first fraction tell you? (Signal.) *6 parts in each whole.*
b. The top number is missing in the first fraction. The fraction equals 1. There are 6 parts in each whole. How many parts do you have to use? (Signal.) *6.*
c. Yes, if there are 6 parts in each whole, you have to use 6 parts to equal 1. Write 6 in the box. ✔
d. What does the bottom number of any fraction tell? (Signal.) *How many parts in each whole.*
e. In the next fraction, the bottom number is missing. What is the top number? (Signal.) *3.*
- The fraction equals 1. Three parts are being used. So how many parts would have to be in each whole? (Signal.) *3.*
f. Yes, if the fraction equals 1 and 3 parts are used, there must be 3 parts in each whole. Write 3 in the box. ✔
g. Work the rest of the problems in Part 2. Fill in the missing numbers so that each fraction equals 1. You have 2 minutes.
- (Observe students and give feedback.)

EXERCISE 3
More, Less, Equal to 1

a. A fraction equals 1 when you use the same number of parts that are in each whole.
- A fraction is more than 1 when you use more parts than are in each whole.
- A fraction is less than 1 when you use less parts than are in each whole.

b. (Write on the board:)

$$\frac{1}{2} \begin{array}{l} \text{more} \\ = \\ \text{less} \end{array}$$

- Does that fraction equal 1? (Signal.) *No.*
- How do you know? (Signal.) *You don't use the same number of parts that are in each whole.*
- In this fraction, how many parts are in each whole? (Signal.) *2.*
- Do you use more than 2 parts or less than 2 parts? (Signal.) *Less.*
- So the fraction is less than 1. I'll circle the word **less.**
- (Circle **less**.)

c. Touch the first problem in Part 3.
- Does that fraction equal 1? (Signal.) *No.*
- How do you know? (Signal.) *You don't use the same number of parts that are in each whole.*
- How many parts are in each whole? (Signal.) *3.*
- Do you use more than 3 parts or less than 3 parts? (Signal.) *More.*
- So is that fraction more or less than 1? (Signal.) *More.*
- Circle the word **more.**

d. Touch the next problem.
- Does that fraction equal 1? (Signal.) *Yes.*
- How do you know? (Signal.) *You use the same number of parts that are in each whole.*
- That fraction equals 1, so circle the **equals.**

e. Touch the next problem.
- Does that fraction equal 1? (Signal.) *No.*
- How do you know? (Signal.) *You don't use the same number of parts that are in each whole.*
- How many parts are in each whole? (Signal.) *6.*
- Do you use more than 6 parts or less than 6 parts? (Signal.) *Less.*

- So is that fraction more than 1 or less than 1? (Signal.) *Less.*
- Circle the word **less.** ✔
f. Work the rest of the problems in Part 3 the same way. You have 5 minutes.
- (Observe students and give feedback.)

EXERCISE 4

Workcheck

a. We're going to check the answers. Exchange workbooks, and get ready to check the answers. (Pause.)
- Put an **X** next to each problem that the person misses.
- (Check and correct. See **Answer Key**.)
- Return the workbooks.

b. Now we're going to figure out the number of points you've earned for this lesson.
- (Point to the posted information.)

Worksheet Items	Errors	Points
	0–2	10
	3	7
	4	5
	5	3
	6	1
	7 or more	0

- Count the number of items you got wrong. Figure out the number of points you earned and write the number in the "Items" box.
- (Observe students and give feedback.)

c. (Tell the group how many points they earned for the lesson.) Write that number in the "Hard Work" box; then figure out the total for today's lesson.

d. Turn to the Point Summary Charts. Write the points in the box for Lesson 12. ✔

EXERCISE 1

Making Fractions Equal 1

a. Turn to Lesson 13 in your workbook. Touch the first problem in Part 1.
- All the fractions in this part equal 1, but part of each fraction is missing. You have to fill in the missing part. What does the bottom number of the first fraction tell you? (Signal.) *7 parts in each whole.*

b. The top number is missing in the first fraction. The fraction equals 1. There are 7 parts in each whole. How many parts do you have to use? (Signal.) *7.*

c. Yes, if there are 7 parts in each whole, you have to use 7 parts to equal 1. Write 7 in the box. ✔

d. What does the bottom number of a fraction tell? (Signal.) *How many parts in each whole.*

e. In the next fraction, the bottom number is missing. What is the top number? (Signal.) *5.*
- The fraction equals 1. 5 parts are being used. So how many parts would have to be in each whole? (Signal.) *5.*

f. Yes, if the fraction equals 1 and 5 parts are used, there must be 5 parts in each whole. Write 5 in the box. ✔

g. Work the rest of the problems in Part 1. Fill in the missing numbers so that each fraction equals 1. You have 2 minutes.
- (Observe students and give feedback.)

EXERCISE 2

More, Less, Equal to 1

a. A fraction equals 1 when you use the same number of parts that are in each whole.
- A fraction is more than 1 when you use more parts than are in each whole.
- A fraction is less than 1 when you use less parts than are in each whole.

b. (Write on the board:)

$$\frac{7}{5} \genfrac{}{}{0pt}{}{\text{more}}{\text{less}} = 1$$

- Does that fraction equal 1? (Signal.) *No.*
- How do you know? (Signal.) *You don't use the same number of parts that are in each whole.*
- In this fraction, how many parts are in each whole? (Signal.) *5.*
- Do you use more than 5 parts or less than 5 parts? (Signal.) *More.*
- So is the fraction more than 1 or less than 1? (Signal.) *More.*

c. Touch the first problem in Part 2.
- Does that fraction equal 1? (Signal.) *No.*
- How do you know? (Signal.) *You don't use the same number of parts that are in each whole.*
- How many parts are in each whole? (Signal.) *8.*
- Do you use more than 8 parts or less than 8 parts? (Signal.) *Less.*
- So is that fraction more or less than 1? (Signal.) *Less.*
- Circle the word **less.** ✔

d. Touch the next problem.
- Does that fraction equal 1? (Signal.) *Yes.*
- How do you know? (Signal.) *You use the same number of parts that are in each whole.*
- That fraction equals 1 so circle the **equals.** ✔

e. Touch the next problem.
- Does that fraction equal 1? (Signal.) *No.*
- How do you know? (Signal.) *You don't use the same number of parts that are in each whole.*
- How many parts are in each whole? (Signal.) *6.*
- Do you use more than 6 parts or less than 6 parts? (Signal.) *More.*
- So is that fraction more or less than 1? (Signal.) *More.*
- Circle the word **more.**

f. Work the rest of the problems in Part 2 the same way. You have 2 minutes.
- (Observe students and give feedback.)

EXERCISE 3

Addition/Subtraction

a. (Write on the board:)
★

$$1 = \frac{7-\square}{5} = \frac{\square}{\square}$$

$$1 = \frac{3+\square}{7} = \frac{\square}{\square}$$

- The fractions on the board are equal to 1, but part of each fraction is missing. We have to fill in the missing part.
- (Touch the denominator 5 in the first fraction.)
- What does this number tell you? (Signal.) *5 parts in each whole.*

b. The fraction equals 1. There are 5 parts in each whole. So how many parts do we have to use? (Signal.) *5.*
- Is the top number 5? (Signal.) *No.*
- We have to fix the top of the fraction so that it equals 5.
- (Touch as you read.) 7 minus how many equals 5? How many do I have to minus from 7 to equal 5? (Signal.) *2.*
- Yes, 2.

c. (Write 2 in the box.)

$$1 = \frac{7-\boxed{2}}{5} = \frac{\square}{\square}$$

- Now the top equals 5. So here is how I rewrite the fraction.
- (Write on the board:)

$$1 = \frac{7-\boxed{2}}{5} = \frac{\boxed{5}}{\boxed{5}}$$

d. (Touch the next fraction.)

$$1 = \frac{3+\square}{7} = \frac{\square}{\square}$$

- This fraction equals 1. Let's figure out the missing part.
- (Touch the denominator 7 in the second fraction.)
- What does this number tell you? (Signal.) *7 parts in each whole.*

e. The fraction equals 1. There are 7 parts in each whole. So how many parts do we have to use? (Signal.) *7.*
- Is the top number 7? (Signal.) *No.*
- We have to fix the top of the fraction so that it equals 7.
- (Touch as you read.) 3 plus how many equals 7? How many do I have to add to 3 to equal 7? (Signal.) *4.*
- Yes, 4.

f. (Write to show:)

$$1 = \frac{3+\boxed{4}}{7} = \frac{\square}{\square}$$

- Now the top equals 7. I'll write the fraction in the next box.

g. (Write 4 in the box.)

$$1 = \frac{3+\boxed{4}}{7} = \frac{\boxed{7}}{\boxed{7}}$$

h. Find Part 3 on your worksheet.
- All of the fractions in Part 3 are equal to 1, but part of each fraction is missing. You have to fill in the missing part.

i. Touch the first problem in Part 3.
- What does the bottom number tell you? (Signal.) *8 parts in each whole.*
- The fraction equals 1. So how many parts do you have to use? (Signal.) *8.*
- Is the top number 8? (Signal.) *No.*
- You have to fix the top of the fraction so that it equals 8.

- How many do you have to add to 3? (Signal.) *5.*
- Yes, 5. Write the 5.
- Now the top number equals 8. Write the fraction in the next box. ✔
j. Work the rest of the problems in Part 3 the same way. You have 6 minutes.
- (Observe students and give feedback.)

EXERCISE 4

Workcheck

a. We're going to check the answers. Exchange workbooks, and get ready to check the answers. (Pause.)
- Put an **X** next to each problem that the person misses.
- (Check and correct. See *Answer Key*.)
- Return the workbooks.

b. Now we're going to figure out the number of points you've earned for this lesson.
- (Point to the posted information.)

Worksheet Items	Errors	Points
	0–2	10
	3	7
	4	5
	5	3
	6	1
	7 or more	0

- Count the number of items you got wrong. Figure out the number of points you earned and write the number in the "Items" box.
- (Observe students and give feedback.)
c. (Tell the group how many points they earned for the lesson.) Write that number in the "Hard Work" box; then figure out the total for today's lesson.
d. Turn to the Point Summary Charts. Write the points in the box for Lesson 13. ✔

EXERCISE 1

Making Fractions Equal 1

a. Turn to Lesson 14 in your workbook. Touch the first problem in Part 1.
- All the fractions in this part equal 1, but part of each fraction is missing. You have to fill in the missing part. What does the bottom number of the first fraction tell you? (Signal.) *8 parts in each whole.*

b. The top number is missing in the first fraction. The fraction equals 1. There are 8 parts in each whole. How many parts do you have to use? (Signal.) *8.*

c. Yes, if there are 8 parts in each whole, you have to use 8 parts. Write 8 in the box. ✔

d. Work the rest of the problems in Part 1. Fill in the missing numbers. You have 2 minutes.
- (Observe students and give feedback.)

EXERCISE 2

More, Less, Equal to 1

a. Find Part 2 on your worksheet. Touch the first problem.
- Does that fraction equal 1? (Signal.) *No.*
- How do you know? (Signal.) *You don't use the same number of parts that are in each whole.*
- How many parts are in each whole? (Signal.) *7.*
- Do you use more than 7 parts or less than 7 parts? (Signal.) *Less.*
- So is that fraction more or less than 1? (Signal.) *Less.*
- Circle the word **less.**

b. Touch the next problem
- Does that fraction equal 1? (Signal.) *Yes.*
- How do you know? (Signal.) *You use the same number of parts that are in each whole.*
- The fraction equals 1, so circle the **equals** sign.

c. Work the rest of the problems in Part 2 the same way. You have 2 minutes.
- (Observe students and give feedback.)

EXERCISE 3

Addition/Subtraction

a. (Write on the board:)
★

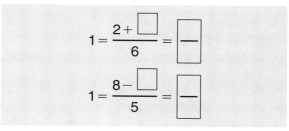

- The fractions on the board are equal to 1, but part of each fraction is missing. We have to fill in the missing part.
- (Touch the denominator 6 in the first fraction.)
- What does this number tell you? (Signal.) *6 parts in each whole.*

b. The fraction equals 1. There are 6 parts in each whole. So how many parts do we have to use? (Signal.) *6.*
- Is the top number 6? (Signal.) *No.*
- We have to fix the top of the fraction so that it equals 6.
- (Touch as you read.) 2 plus how many equals 6? How many do I have to add to 2 to equal 6? (Signal.) *4.*
- Yes, 4.
- (Write to show:)

$$1 = \frac{2 + \boxed{4}}{6} = \boxed{\frac{}{}}$$

- Now the top equals 6. So here is how I rewrite the fraction.

- (Write to show:)

$$1 = \frac{2 + \boxed{4}}{6} = \boxed{\frac{6}{6}}$$

c. (Touch the next fraction.)

$$1 = \frac{8 - \boxed{}}{5} = \boxed{}$$

- This fraction equals 1. Let's figure out the missing part.
- (Touch the denominator 5 in the second fraction.)
- What does this number tell you? (Signal.) *5 parts in each whole.*
- The fraction equals 1. There are 5 parts in each whole. So how many parts do we have to use? (Signal.) *5.*
- Is the top number 5? (Signal.) *No.*
- We have to fix the top of the fraction so that it equals 5.
- (Touch as you read.) 8 minus how many equals 5? How many do I have to minus from 8 to equal 5? (Signal.) *3.*
- Yes, 3.
- (Write to show:)

$$1 = \frac{8 - \boxed{3}}{5} = \boxed{\frac{}{}}$$

- Now the top equals 5. I'll write the fraction in the next box.
- (Write on the board:)

$$1 = \frac{8 - \boxed{3}}{5} = \boxed{\frac{5}{5}}$$

d. Find Part 3 on your worksheet.
- All of the fractions in Part 3 are equal to 1, but part of each fraction is missing. You have to fill in the missing part.
- Touch the first problem in Part 3.

- What does the bottom number tell you? (Signal.) *6 parts in each whole.*
- The fraction equals 1. So how many parts do you have to use? (Signal.) *6.*
- Is the top number 6? (Signal.) *No.*
- You have to fix the top of the fraction so that it equals 6.
- How many do you have to add to 3? (Signal.) *3.*
- Yes, 3. Write the 3.
- Now the top number equals 6. Write the fraction in the next box. ✔

e. Work the rest of the problems in Part 3 the same way. You have 5 minutes.
- (Observe students and give feedback.)

EXERCISE 4
Fraction Naming

a. (*Before the lesson, write on the board:)
★

$$\frac{1}{2} \quad \frac{2}{7} \quad \frac{3}{5} \quad \frac{5}{6} \quad \frac{7}{3} \quad \frac{3}{2} \quad \frac{2}{9} \quad \frac{10}{8}$$

b. Let's go over the names of the fractions that we learned.
- Read each fraction when I touch it. (Touch each fraction.)
- (Repeat any that are difficult.)

EXERCISE 5
Workcheck

a. We're going to check the answers. Exchange workbooks, and get ready to check the answers. (Pause.)
- Put an **X** next to each problem that the person misses.
- (Check and correct. See **Answer Key**.)
- Return the workbooks.
b. Now we're going to figure out the number of points you've earned for this lesson.

- (Point to the posted information.)

Worksheet Items	Errors	Points
	0–2	10
	3	7
	4	5
	5	3
	6	1
	7 or more	0

- Count the number of items you got wrong. Figure out the number of points you earned and write the number in the "Items" box.
- (Observe students and give feedback.)

c. (Tell the group how many points they earned for the lesson.) Write that number in the "Hard Work" box; then figure out the total for today's lesson.

d. Turn to the Point Summary Charts. Write the points in the box for Lesson 14. ✔

EXERCISE 1

More, Less, Equal to 1

a. Turn to Lesson 15 in your workbook. Look at the first problem in Part 1.
- Does that fraction equal 1? (Signal.) *No.*
- How do you know? (Signal.) *You don't use the same number of parts that are in each whole.*
- How many parts are in each whole? (Signal.) *4.*
- Do you use more than 4 parts or less than 4 parts? (Signal.) *More.*
- So is that fraction more or less than 1? (Signal.) *More.*
- Circle the word **more.**

b. Touch the next problem.
- Does that fraction equal 1? (Signal.) *No.*
- How do you know? (Signal.) *You don't use the same number of parts that are in each whole.*
- How many parts are in each whole? (Signal.) *6.*
- Do you use more than 6 parts or less than 6 parts? (Signal.) *Less.*
- So is that fraction more or less than 1? (Signal.) *Less.*

c. Circle the word **less.** Then work the rest of the problems in Part 1. You have 1 minute.
- (Observe students and give feedback.)

EXERCISE 2

Addition/Subtraction

a. (Write on the board:)
★

$$1 = \frac{7 - \boxed{}}{4} = \boxed{\frac{}{}}$$

- The fraction on the board is equal to 1, but part of the fraction is missing. We have to fill in the missing part.
- (Touch the denominator 4 in the fraction.)
- What does this number tell you? (Signal.) *4 parts in each whole.*

b. The fraction equals 1. There are 4 parts in each whole. So how many parts do we have to use? (Signal.) *4.*
- Is the top number 4? (Signal.) *No.*
- We have to fix the top of the fraction so that it equals 4.
- (Touch as you read.) 7 minus how many equals 4? How many do I have to minus from 7 to equal 4? (Signal.) *3.*
- Yes, 3.

c. (Write 3 in the box.)

$$1 = \frac{7 - \boxed{3}}{4} = \boxed{\frac{}{}}$$

- Now the top equals 4. I'll write the fraction in the next box.
- (Write to show:)

$$1 = \frac{7 - \boxed{3}}{4} = \boxed{\frac{4}{4}}$$

d. Find Part 2 on your worksheet.
- All of the fractions in Part 2 are equal to 1, but part of each fraction is missing. You have to fill in the missing part.

e. Touch the first problem in Part 2.
- What does the bottom number tell you? (Signal.) *8 parts in each whole.*
- The fraction equals 1. So how many parts do we have to use? (Signal.) *8.*
- Is the top number 8? (Signal.) *No.*
- You have to fix the top of the fraction so that it equals 8.
- How many do you have to subtract from ten? (Signal.) *2.*
- Yes, 2. Write the 2.
- Now the top number equals 8. Write the fraction in the next box. ✔

f. Work the rest of the problems in Part 2 the same way. You have 2 minutes.
- (Observe students and give feedback.)

EXERCISE 3

Addition/Subtraction

a. (Draw on the board:)

★

- We're going to write the fraction for this picture. We're going to use a plus sign to show the different parts.
- Tell me how many parts are in each whole. Get ready. (Signal.) *3.*
- So I'll write a 3 on the bottom.
- (Write to show:)

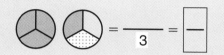

b. Some of the parts that are used are shaded and some are dotted. Count all the shaded parts. (Pause.)
- How many parts are shaded? (Signal.) *4.*
- So I'll write a 4 on the top.
- (Write to show:)

c. Now I'm going to add the parts that are dotted, so I write a plus sign.
- (Write to show:)

- Count all the dotted parts. (Pause.)
- How many parts are dotted? (Signal.) *1.*
- So I'll write a 1 after the plus sign.
- (Write to show:)

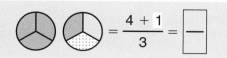

d. Now I'll rewrite the fraction. How much does 4 plus 1 equal? (Signal.) *5.*
- (Write to show:)

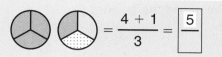

- What do I write on the bottom? (Signal.) *3.*
- (Write to show:)

- Read the answer. (Signal.) *5 thirds.*

e. Touch the first problem in Part 3.
- You're going to write the fraction for that picture and use a plus sign to show the different parts.
- Tell me how many parts are in each whole. Get ready. (Signal.) *5.*
- Where do you write the 5? (Signal.) *On the bottom.*
- Write it. ✔
- Where will you write the number for the parts that are used? (Signal.) *On the top.*
- How many parts are shaded? (Signal.) *3.*
- Write 3. Then write the plus sign. ✔
- How many parts are dotted? (Signal.) *4.*
- Write 4. ✔
- Now you have to rewrite the fraction. How much does 3 plus 4 equal? (Signal.) *7.*
- Write the 7 in the top of the box. ✔
- What do you write in the bottom? (Signal.) *5.*
- Write 5. ✔
- What is the complete fraction? (Signal.) *7 fifths.*

f. Work the rest of the problems in Part 3 the same way. You have 6 minutes.
- (Observe students and give feedback.)

EXERCISE 4

Fraction Naming

a. (Write on the board:)

★

$$\frac{3}{5} \quad \frac{7}{8} \quad \frac{2}{3} \quad \frac{1}{2} \quad \frac{5}{9}$$

$$\frac{6}{7} \quad \frac{3}{2} \quad \frac{5}{6} \quad \frac{5}{4} \quad \frac{7}{10}$$

- Let's go over the names of the fractions that we learned.
- Read each fraction when I touch it. (Touch each fraction.)
- (Repeat any that are difficult.)

EXERCISE 5

Workcheck

a. We're going to check the answers. Exchange workbooks, and get ready to check the answers. (Pause.)
- Put an **X** next to each item that the person misses.
- (Check and correct. See *Answer Key*.)
- Return the workbooks.

b. Now we're going to figure out the number of points you've earned for this lesson.
- (Point to the posted information.)

Worksheet Items	Errors	Points
	0–2	10
	3	7
	4	5
	5	3
	6	1
	7 or more	0

- Count the number of items you got wrong. Figure out the number of points you earned and write the number in the "Items" box.
- (Observe students and give feedback.)

c. (Tell the group how many points they earned for the lesson.) Write that number in the "Hard Work" box; then figure out the total for today's lesson.

d. Turn to the Point Summary Charts. Write the points in the box for Lesson 15. ✔

e. Total your points for Lessons 11 through 15 and write the total number on the chart.
- (Observe students and give feedback.)

f. Everybody, find the Five-Lesson Point Graph. ✔
- (Help the students plot their five-lesson scores on the graph.)

Lesson 16

Skipping Note: Check the students' errors from Lesson 15. If no more than 1 fourth of the students made more than 4 errors, skip this lesson and proceed with Lesson 17.

EXERCISE 1

More, Less, Equal to 1

a. Turn to Lesson 16 in your workbook.
- Touch the first problem in Part 1.
- Does that fraction equal 1? (Signal.) *No.*
- How do you know? (Signal.) *You don't use the same number of parts that are in each whole.*
- How many parts are in each whole? (Signal.) *9.*
- Do you use more than 9 parts or less than 9 parts? (Signal.) *Less.*
- So is that fraction more or less than 1? (Signal.) *Less.*
- Circle the word **less.**

b. Work the rest of the problems in Part 1. You have 2 minutes.
- (Observe students and give feedback.)

EXERCISE 2

Addition/Subtraction— No Pictures

a. (Write on the board:)
★

$$1 = \frac{7 - \boxed{}}{5} = \boxed{\frac{}{}}$$

- The fraction on the board is equal to 1, but part of the fraction is missing. We have to fill in the missing part.
- (Touch the denominator 5 in the fraction.)
- What does this number tell you? (Signal.) *5 parts in each whole.*

b. The fraction equals 1. There are 5 parts in each whole. So how many parts do we have to use? (Signal.) *5.*

- Is the top number 5? (Signal.) *No.*
- We have to fix the top of the fraction so that it equals 5.
- (Touch as you read.) 7 minus how many equals 5? How many do I have to minus from 7 to equal 5? (Signal.) *2.*
- Yes, 2.
- (Write 2 in the box:)

$$1 = \frac{7 - \boxed{2}}{5} = \boxed{\frac{}{}}$$

- Now the top equals 5. I'll write the fraction in the next box.
- (Write to show:)

$$1 = \frac{7 - \boxed{2}}{5} = \boxed{\frac{5}{5}}$$

c. Find Part 2 on your worksheet.
- All of the fractions in Part 2 are equal to 1, but part of each fraction is missing. You have to fill in the missing part.
- Touch the first problem in Part 2.
- What does the bottom number tell you? (Signal.) *7 parts in each whole.*
- The fraction equals 1. So how many parts do we have to use? (Signal.) *7.*
- Is the top number 7? (Signal.) *No.*
- You have to fix the top of the fraction so that it equals 7.
- How many do you have to subtract from ten? (Signal.) *3.*
- Yes, 3. Write the 3. ✔
- Now the top number equals 7. Write the fraction in the next box. ✔

d. Work the rest of the problems in Part 2. You have 2 minutes.
- (Observe students and give feedback.)

EXERCISE 3

Addition/Subtraction

a. (Draw on the board:)
★

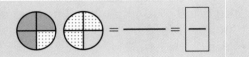

- We're going to write the fraction for this picture. We're going to use a plus sign to show the different parts.
- Tell me how many parts are in each whole. Get ready. (Signal.) *4.*
- So I'll write a 4 on the bottom.
- (Write to show:)

$$\bigcirc\bigcirc = \dfrac{}{4} = \dfrac{}{}$$

b. Some of the parts that are used are shaded and some are dotted. Count all the shaded parts. (Pause.)
- How many parts are shaded? (Signal.) *3.*
- So I'll write a 3 on the top.
- (Write to show:)

$$\bigcirc\bigcirc = \dfrac{3}{4} = \dfrac{}{}$$

c. Now I'm going to add the parts that are dotted, so I write a plus sign.
- (Write to show:)

$$\bigcirc\bigcirc = \dfrac{3 +}{4} = \dfrac{}{}$$

- Count all the dotted parts. (Pause.)
- How many parts are dotted? (Signal.) *4.*
- So I'll write a 4 after the plus sign.
- (Write to show:)

$$\bigcirc\bigcirc = \dfrac{3 + 4}{4} = \dfrac{}{}$$

d. Now I'll rewrite the fraction. How much does 3 plus 4 equal? (Signal.) *7.*
- (Write to show:)

$$\bigcirc\bigcirc = \dfrac{3 + 4}{4} = \boxed{7}$$

- What do I write on the bottom? (Signal.) *4.*
- (Write to show:)

$$\bigcirc\bigcirc = \dfrac{3 + 4}{4} = \boxed{\dfrac{7}{4}}$$

- Read the answer. (Signal.) *7 fourths.*

e. Touch the first problem in Part 3.
- You're going to write the fraction for this picture and use a plus sign to show the different parts.
- Tell me how many parts are in each whole. Get ready. (Signal.) *6.*
- Where do you write the 6? (Signal.) *On the bottom.*

f. Where will you write the number for the parts that are used? (Signal.) *On the top.*
- How many parts are shaded? (Signal.) *2.*
- Write 2. Then write the plus sign. ✔
- How many parts are dotted? (Signal.) *3.*
- Write 3. ✔
- Now you have to rewrite the fraction. How much does 2 plus 3 equal? (Signal.) *5.*
- Tell me the complete fraction you will write in the box. (Signal.) *5 sixths.*
- Write it. ✔

g. Work the rest of the problems in Part 3 the same way. You have 6 minutes.
- (Observe students and give feedback.)

EXERCISE 4

Fraction Naming

a. (*Before the lesson, write on the board:)

★
$$\frac{2}{3} \quad \frac{5}{2} \quad \frac{3}{7} \quad \frac{6}{10} \quad \frac{5}{9} \quad \frac{6}{5} \quad \frac{1}{2} \quad \frac{7}{5} \quad \frac{8}{3}$$

- Let's go over the names of the fractions that we learned.
- Read each fraction when I touch it. (Touch each fraction.)
- (Repeat any that are difficult.)

EXERCISE 5

Workcheck

a. We're going to check the answers. Exchange workbooks, and get ready to check the answers. (Pause.)

- Put an **X** next to each item that the person misses.
- (Check and correct. See **Answer Key**.)
- Return the workbooks.

b. Now we're going to figure out the number of points you've earned for this lesson.

- (Point to the posted information.)

Worksheet Items	Errors	Points
	0–2	10
	3	7
	4	5
	5	3
	6	1
	7 or more	0

- Count the number of items you got wrong. Figure out the number of points you earned and write the number in the "Items" box.
- (Observe students and give feedback.)

c. (Tell the group how many points they earned for the lesson.) Write that number in the "Hard Work" box; then figure out the total for today's lesson.

d. Turn to the Point Summary Charts. Write the points in the box for Lesson 16. ✔

EXERCISE 1

Addition/Subtraction

a. (Draw on the board:)

★

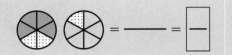

- We're going to write the fraction for this picture. We're going to use a plus sign to show the different parts.
- Tell me how many parts are in each whole. Get ready. (Signal.) *6.*
- So I'll write a 6 on the bottom.
- (Write to show:)

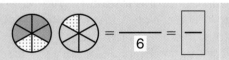

b. Some of the parts that are used are shaded and some are dotted. Count all the shaded parts. (Pause.)
- How many parts are shaded? (Signal.) *4.*
- So I'll write a 4 on the top.
- (Write to show:)

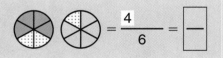

c. Now I'm going to add the parts that are dotted, so I write a plus sign.
- (Write to show:)

$$\bigcirc\bigcirc = \frac{4 +}{6} = \boxed{}$$

- Count all the dotted parts. (Pause.)
- How many parts are dotted? (Signal.) *3.*
- So I'll write a 3 after the plus sign.
- (Write to show:)

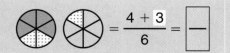

d. Now I'll rewrite the fraction. How much does 4 plus 3 equal? (Signal.) *7.*
- Tell me the complete fraction to write in the box. (Signal.) *7 sixths.*
- (Write to show:)

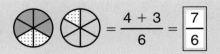

e. Turn to Lesson 17. Touch the first problem in Part 1.
- You're going to write the fraction for this picture and use a plus sign to show the different parts.
- Tell me how many parts are in each whole. Get ready. (Signal.) *6.*
- Where do you write the 6? (Signal.) *On the bottom.*
- Where will you write the number for the parts that are used? (Signal.) *On the top.*
- Tell me how many parts are shaded. Get ready. (Signal.) *4.*
- Write it. Then write the plus sign. ✔
- Tell me how many parts are dotted. Get ready. (Signal.) *2.*
- Write it. ✔

f. Now you have to rewrite the fraction. How much does 4 plus 2 equal? (Signal.) *6.*
- Tell me the complete fraction you will write in the box. (Signal.) *6 sixths.*
- Write it. ✔

g. Work the rest of the problems in Part 1 the same way. You have 3 minutes.
- (Observe students and give feedback.)

EXERCISE 2

Addition/Subtraction

a. (Write on the board:)

★

$$\frac{2}{5} + \frac{6}{5} \qquad \frac{2}{3} + \frac{1}{2}$$

$$\frac{4}{8} + \frac{8}{4} \qquad \frac{2}{6} + \frac{1}{6}$$

- You can rewrite some of these fractions that are added or subtracted. Here's the rule. You can rewrite fractions when the wholes are the same.
- When can you rewrite fractions that are added or subtracted? (Signal.) *When the wholes are the same.*
- (Repeat until firm.)

b. (Point to $\frac{2}{5} + \frac{6}{5}$.)

- The wholes are the same for these fractions. The wholes are the same because the first fraction has 5 parts in each whole and the other fraction has 5 parts in each whole.

c. (Point to $\frac{2}{3} + \frac{1}{2}$.)

- Are the wholes the same for these fractions? (Signal.) *No.*
- The wholes are not the same because the first fraction (touch $\frac{2}{3}$) has 3 parts in each whole and the other fraction (touch $\frac{1}{2}$) has 2 parts in each whole.

d. (Point to $\frac{4}{8} + \frac{8}{4}$.)

- Are the wholes the same for these fractions? (Signal.) *No.*
- The wholes are not the same because the first fraction (touch $\frac{4}{8}$) has 8 parts in each whole and the other fraction (touch $\frac{8}{4}$) has 4 parts in each whole.

e. (Point to $\frac{2}{6} + \frac{1}{6}$.)

- Are the wholes the same for these fractions? (Signal.) *Yes.*
- The wholes are the same because the first fraction has 6 parts in each whole and the other fraction has 6 parts in each whole.

f. Remember, you can rewrite fractions that are added or subtracted when the wholes are the same.
- (Write on the board:)

$$\frac{2}{3} + \frac{5}{3}$$

- Are the wholes the same for these fractions? (Signal.) *Yes.*
- When can you rewrite fractions that are added or subtracted? (Signal.) *When the wholes are the same.*
- The wholes are the same, so I can write the fraction with only one 3.
- (Write to show:)

$$\frac{2}{3} + \frac{5}{3} = \frac{2 + 5}{3}$$

g. (Write on the board:)

$$\frac{1}{4} + \frac{3}{5} =$$

- Are the wholes the same for these fractions? (Signal.) *No.*
- The wholes are not the same, so I can't rewrite the fraction.

h. (Write on the board:)

$$\frac{3}{2} + \frac{6}{2} =$$

- Are the wholes the same for these fractions? (Signal.) *Yes.*
- When can you rewrite fractions that are added or subtracted? (Signal.) *When the wholes are the same.*
- The wholes are the same, so I can write the fraction with only one 2.
- (Write to show:)

$$\frac{3}{2} + \frac{6}{2} = \frac{3 + 6}{2}$$

i. (Write on the board:)

$$\frac{5}{6} - \frac{2}{6} =$$

- Are the wholes the same for these fractions? (Signal.) *Yes.*
- The wholes are the same, so I can write the fraction with only one 6.
- When can you rewrite fractions that are added or subtracted? (Signal.) *When the wholes are the same.*
- (Write to show:)

$$\frac{5}{6} - \frac{2}{6} = \boxed{\frac{5-2}{6}}$$

j. (Write on the board:)

$$\frac{8}{7} - \frac{5}{7}$$

- Can I rewrite these fractions? (Signal.) *Yes.*
- How do you know? (Signal.) *The wholes are the same.*
- Right. The wholes are the same. Tell me what to write on the bottom of the fraction. (Signal.) *7.*
- (Write to show:)

$$\frac{8}{7} - \frac{5}{7} = \frac{\boxed{}}{7}$$

- Tell me what to write on the top of the fraction. (Signal.) *8 minus 5.*
- (Write to show:)

$$\frac{8}{7} - \frac{5}{7} = \frac{8-5}{7}$$

k. (Write on the board:)

$$\frac{3}{9} - \frac{2}{7}$$

- Can I rewrite these fractions? (Signal.) *No.*
- How do you know? (Signal.) *The wholes are not the same.*

EXERCISE 3
Addition/Subtraction

a. Touch the first problem in Part 2.
- Can you rewrite the fractions in that problem? (Signal.) *Yes.*
- How do you know? (Signal.) *The wholes are the same.*
- When you rewrite those fractions, what will you write on the bottom? (Signal.) *3.*
- What will you write on the top? (Signal.) *2 plus 4.*
- Rewrite that fraction. ✔
- Now you have to write the fraction in the box. How much does 2 plus 4 equal? (Signal.) *6.*
- Tell me the complete fraction you will write in the box. (Signal.) *6 thirds.*
- Write it. ✔
b. Touch the next problem.
- Can you rewrite those fractions? (Signal.) *No.*
- How do you know? (Signal.) *The wholes are not the same.*
- You can't do anything to that problem. You just skip it.
c. Work the rest of the problems in Part 2. Remember, if you can't rewrite the fractions, skip the problem. You have 6 minutes.
- (Observe students and give feedback.)

EXERCISE 4
Workcheck

a. We're going to check the answers. Exchange workbooks, and get ready to check the answers. (Pause.)
- Put an **X** next to each problem that the person misses.
- (Check and correct. See **Answer Key.**)
- Return the workbooks.

b. Now we're going to figure out the number of points you've earned for this lesson.
- (Point to the posted information.)

Worksheet Items	Errors	Points
	0–2	10
	3	7
	4	5
	5	3
	6	1
	7 or more	0

- Count the number of items you got wrong. Figure out the number of points you earned and write the number in the "Items" box.
- (Observe students and give feedback.)

c. (Tell the group how many points they earned for the lesson.) Write that number in the "Hard Work" box; then figure out the total for today's lesson.

d. Turn to the Point Summary Charts. Write the points in the box for Lesson 17. ✔

Skipping Note: Check the students' errors from Lesson 17. If no more than 1 fourth of the students made more than 4 errors, skip this lesson and proceed with Lesson 19.

EXERCISE 1

More, Less, Equal to 1

a. Turn to Lesson 18.
- Touch the first problem in Part 1.
- Does that fraction equal 1? (Signal.) *No.*
- How do you know? (Signal.) *You don't use the same number of parts that are in each whole.*
- How many parts are in each whole? (Signal.) *5.*
- Do you use more than 5 parts or less than 5 parts? (Signal.) *More.*
- So is that fraction more or less than 1? (Signal.) *More.*
- Circle the word **more.**

b. Touch the next problem.
- Does that fraction equal 1? (Signal.) *Yes.*
- How do you know? (Signal.) *You use the same number of parts that are in each whole.*
- Circle the **equals** sign.

c. Work the rest of the problems in Part 1 the same way. You have 2 minutes.
- (Observe students and give feedback.)

EXERCISE 2

Addition/Subtraction

a. Find Part 2 on your worksheet.
- All of the fractions in Part 2 are equal to 1, but part of each fraction is missing. You have to fill in the missing part.

b. Touch the first problem in Part 2.
- What does the bottom number tell you? (Signal.) *7 parts in each whole.*
- The fraction equals 1. So how many parts do we have to use? (Signal.) *7.*
- Is the top number 7? (Signal.) *No.*

- You have to fix the top of the fraction so that it equals 7.
- How many do you have to add to 1? (Signal.) *6.*
- Yes, 6. Write the 6. ✔
- Now the top number equals 7. Tell me the complete fraction you will write in the next box. (Signal.) *7 sevenths.*
- Write it. ✔

c. Work the rest of the problems in Part 2 in the same way. You have 3 minutes.
- (Observe students and give feedback.)

EXERCISE 3

Addition/Subtraction

a. (*Before the lesson, write on the board:)
★
$$\frac{2}{8} + \frac{5}{8} \qquad \frac{2}{3} + \frac{3}{4} \qquad \frac{6}{5} - \frac{5}{6}$$

- You can rewrite some fractions that are added or subtracted. Here's the rule. You can rewrite fractions when the wholes are the same.
- When can you rewrite fractions that are added or subtracted? (Signal.) *When the wholes are the same.*
- (Repeat until firm.)

b. (Point to $\frac{2}{8} + \frac{5}{8}$.)
- Are the wholes the same for these fractions? (Signal.) *Yes.*
- The wholes are the same because the first fraction has 8 parts in each whole and the other fraction has 8 parts in each whole.

c. (Point to $\frac{2}{3} + \frac{3}{4}$.)
- Are the wholes the same for these fractions? (Signal.) *No.*
- The wholes are not the same because the first fraction has 3 parts in each whole and the other fraction has 4 parts in each whole.

d. (Point to $\frac{6}{5} - \frac{5}{6}$.)

- Are the wholes the same for these fractions? (Signal.) *No.*
- Remember, you can rewrite fractions that are added or subtracted when the wholes are the same.

e. (Write on the board:)

$$\frac{6}{5} - \frac{3}{5}$$

- Are the wholes the same for these fractions? (Signal.) *Yes.*
- When can you rewrite fractions that are added or subtracted? (Signal.) *When the wholes are the same.*
- The wholes are the same, so I can write the fraction with only one 5.
- (Write to show:)

$$\frac{6}{5} - \frac{3}{5} = \frac{6 - 3}{5}$$

f. (Write on the board:)

$$\frac{9}{6} + \frac{4}{8}$$

- Are the wholes the same for these fractions? (Signal.) *No.*
- The wholes are not the same, so I can't rewrite the fraction.
- When can you rewrite fractions that are added or subtracted? (Signal.) *When the wholes are the same.*

g. (Write on the board:)

$$\frac{6}{4} - \frac{1}{4}$$

- Can I rewrite these fractions? (Signal.) *Yes.*
- How do you know? (Signal.) *The wholes are the same.*
- Right. The wholes are the same. Tell me what to write on the bottom of the fraction. (Signal.) *4.*

- (Write to show:)

$$\frac{6}{4} - \frac{1}{4} = \frac{}{4}$$

- Tell me what to write on the top of the fraction. (Signal.) *6 minus 1.*
- (Write to show:)

$$\frac{6}{4} - \frac{1}{4} = \frac{6 - 1}{4}$$

h. (Write on the board:)

$$\frac{2}{5} + \frac{3}{4}$$

- Can I rewrite these fractions? (Signal.) *No.*
- How do you know? (Signal.) *The wholes are not the same.*

EXERCISE 4
Addition/Subtraction

a. Touch the first problem in Part 3.
- Can you rewrite the fractions in that problem? (Signal.) *Yes.*
- How do you know? (Signal.) *The wholes are the same.*
- When you rewrite those fractions, what will you write on the bottom? (Signal.) *3.*
- What will you write on the top? (Signal.) *2 plus 3.*
- Rewrite the fractions. ✔
- Now you have to write the fraction in the box. How much does 2 plus 3 equal? (Signal.) *5.*
- Tell me the complete fraction you will write in the box. (Signal.) *5 thirds.*
- Write it. ✔
b. Touch the next problem.
- Can you rewrite the fractions in that problem? (Signal.) *No.*
- How do you know? (Signal.) *The wholes are not the same.*
- You can't do anything to that problem. You just skip it.

c. Work the rest of the problems in Part 3. Remember, if you can't rewrite the fractions, skip the problem. You have 5 minutes.
- (Observe students and give feedback.)

EXERCISE 5

Workcheck

a. We're going to check the answers. Exchange workbooks, and get ready to check the answers. (Pause.)
- Put an **X** next to each problem that the person misses.
- (Check and correct. See *Answer Key.*)
- Return the workbooks.

b. Now we're going to figure out the number of points you've earned for this lesson.

- (Point to the posted information.)

Worksheet Items	Errors	Points
	0–2	10
	3	7
	4	5
	5	3
	6	1
	7 or more	0

- Count the number of items you got wrong. Figure out the number of points you earned and write the number in the "Items" box.
- (Observe students and give feedback.)

c. (Tell the group how many points they earned for the lesson.) Write that number in the "Hard Work" box; then figure out the total for today's lesson.

d. Turn to the Point Summary Charts. Write the points in the box for Lesson 18. ✔

Lesson 19

EXERCISE 1

Addition/Subtraction

a. Turn to Lesson 19 in your workbook. Find Part 1.
- You're going to write the fraction for that picture and use a plus sign.
- Tell me how many parts are in each whole. Get ready. (Signal.) *2.*
- Where do you write the 2? (Signal.) *On the bottom.*
- Write it. ✔
- Where will you write the number for the parts that are used? (Signal.) *On the top.*
- Tell me how many parts are shaded. Get ready. (Signal.) *3.*
- Write it. Then write the plus sign. ✔
- Tell me how many parts are dotted. Get ready. (Signal.) *1.*
- Write it. ✔

b. Now you have to rewrite the fraction. How much does 3 plus 1 equal? (Signal.) *4.*
- Tell me the complete fraction you will write in the box. (Signal.) *4 halves.*
- Write it. ✔

c. Work the rest of the problems in Part 1 the same way. You have 2 minutes.
- (Observe students and give feedback.)

EXERCISE 2

Addition/Subtraction

a. Touch the first problem in Part 2.
- Can you rewrite the fractions in that problem? (Signal.) *Yes.*
- How do you know? (Signal.) *The wholes are the same.*
- When you rewrite those fractions, what will you write on the bottom? (Signal.) *8.*
- What will you write on the top? (Signal.) *10 minus 2.*
- Rewrite the fractions. ✔
- Now you have to write the fraction in the box. How much does 10 minus 2 equal? (Signal.) *8.*

- Tell me the complete fraction you will write in the box. (Signal.) *8 eighths.*
- Write it. ✔

b. Touch the next problem.
- Can you rewrite those fractions? (Signal.) *No.*
- How do you know? (Signal.) *The wholes are not the same.*
- You can't do anything to that problem. You just skip it.

c. Work the rest of the problems in Part 2. Remember, if you can't rewrite the fractions, skip the problem. You have 4 minutes.
- (Observe students and give feedback.)

EXERCISE 3

Numbers as Fractions

a. (Write on the board:)

- In this fraction, how many parts are in each whole? (Signal.) *1.*

b. (Draw 4 circles to show:)

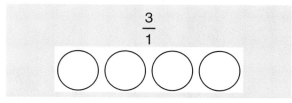

- Each of these wholes has 1 large part.
- (Touch $\frac{3}{1}$.) In this fraction, how many parts are used? (Signal.) *3.*

c. (Color 3 circles to show:)

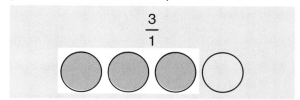

- The fraction 3 over 1 equals how many wholes? (Signal.) *3.*

d. (Write to show:)

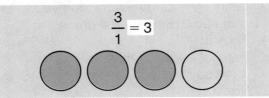

$$\frac{3}{1} = 3$$

e. (Write on the board:)

$$\frac{5}{1}$$

- In this fraction, how many parts are in each whole? (Signal.) *1.*

f. (Draw 5 circles to show:)

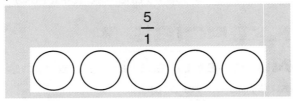

$$\frac{5}{1}$$

- (Touch $\frac{5}{1}$.) In this fraction, how many parts are used? (Signal.) *5.*
- (Color all 5 circles.)
- The fraction 5 over 1 equals how many wholes? (Signal.) *5.*

g. (Write to show:)

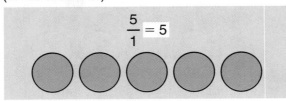

$$\frac{5}{1} = 5$$

- Yes, 5 over 1 equals 5 wholes.

h. See whether you can figure out fractions without the pictures.
- (Write on the board:)

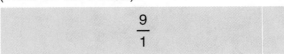

$$\frac{9}{1}$$

- In this fraction, how many parts are in each whole? (Signal.) *1.*
- How many parts are used? (Signal.) *9.*
- The fraction 9 over 1 equals how many wholes? (Signal.) *9.*
- Yes, 9 over 1 equals 9 wholes.

- (Write to show:)

$$\frac{9}{1} = 9$$

i. (Write on the board:)

$$\frac{2}{1}$$

- Tell me how many parts are in each whole. Get ready. (Signal.) *1.*
- How many parts are used? (Signal.) *2.*
- The fraction 2 over 1 equals how many wholes? (Signal.) *2.*
- Yes, 2 over 1 equals 2 wholes.
- (Write to show:)

$$\frac{2}{1} = 2$$

j. (Write on the board:)

$$\frac{4}{1}$$

- Tell me how many parts are in each whole. Get ready. (Signal.) *1.*
- How many parts are used? (Signal.) *4.*
- The fraction 4 over 1 equals how many wholes? (Signal.) *4.*
- Yes, 4 over 1 equals 4 wholes.
- (Write to show:)

$$\frac{4}{1} = 4$$

EXERCISE 4

Numbers as Fractions

a. I'll say some numbers. You tell how to write each number as a fraction.
- How would you write 3 as a fraction? (Signal.) *3 over 1.*
- How would you write 5 as a fraction? (Signal.) *5 over 1.*
- How would you write 6 as a fraction? (Signal.) *6 over 1.*

b. Touch the first problem in Part 3.
- You have to write each number as a fraction.
- How would you write the first number as a fraction? (Signal.) *4 over 1.*
- Touch the next problem.
- How would you write that number as a fraction? (Signal.) *8 over 1.*

c. Write each number in Part 3 as a fraction. You have 3 minutes.
- (Observe students and give feedback.)

EXERCISE 5

Workcheck

a. We're going to check the answers. Exchange workbooks, and get ready to check the answers. (Pause.)
- Put an **X** next to each problem that the person misses.
- (Check and correct. See **Answer Key.**)
- Return the workbooks.

b. Now we're going to figure out the number of points you've earned for this lesson.
- (Point to the posted information.)

Worksheet Items	Errors	Points
	0–2	10
	3	7
	4	5
	5	3
	6	1
	7 or more	0

- Count the number of items you got wrong. Figure out the number of points you earned and write the number in the "Items" box.
- (Observe students and give feedback.)

c. (Tell the group how many points they earned for the lesson.) Write that number in the "Hard Work" box; then figure out the total for today's lesson.

d. Turn to the Point Summary Charts. Write the points in the box for Lesson 19. ✔

EXERCISE 1

More, Less, Equal to 1

a. Turn to Lesson 20 in your workbook.
- Touch the first problem in Part 1.
- Does that fraction equal 1? (Signal.) *No.*
- How do you know? (Signal.) *You don't use the same number of parts that are in each whole.*
- Tell me how many parts are in each whole. Get ready. (Signal.) *4.*
- Do you use more than 4 parts or less than 4 parts? (Signal.) *More.*
- So is that fraction more or less than 1? (Signal.) *More.*
- Circle the word **more**.

b. Work the rest of the problems in Part 1 in the same way. You have 2 minutes.
- (Observe students and give feedback.)

EXERCISE 2

Addition/Subtraction

a. Touch the first problem in Part 2.
- Can you rewrite the fractions in that problem? (Signal.) *Yes.*
- How do you know? (Signal.) *The wholes are the same.*
- When you rewrite those fractions, what will you write on the bottom? (Signal.) *5.*
- What will you write on the top? (Signal.) *7 minus 3.*
- Rewrite the fractions. ✔
- Now you have to write the fraction in the box. How much does 7 minus 3 equal? (Signal.) *4.*
- Tell me the complete fraction you will write in the box. (Signal.) *4 fifths.*
- Write it. ✔

b. Touch the next problem.
- Can you rewrite those fractions? (Signal.) *No.*
- How do you know? (Signal.) *The wholes are not the same.*
- You can't do anything to that problem. You just skip it.

c. Work the rest of the problems in Part 2. Remember, if you can't rewrite the fractions, skip the problem. You have 4 minutes.
- (Observe students and give feedback.)

EXERCISE 3

Addition/Subtraction

a. Look at Part 3.
- You're going to rewrite these fractions and then draw the pictures. When can you rewrite fractions? (Signal.) *When the wholes are the same.*

b. Touch the first problem.
- Can you rewrite the fractions in that problem? (Signal.) *Yes.*
- How do you know? (Signal.) *The wholes are the same.*
- What will you write on the bottom? (Signal.) *3.*
- What will you write on the top? (Signal.) *2 plus 3.*
- Rewrite the fractions. ✔

c. The wholes are the same, so you can make a picture. How many parts in each whole? (Signal.) *3.*
- Make the lines for the parts in each whole. ✔
- Now show how many parts you use. Shade 2 parts. Then make dots for 3 more parts. ✔

d. Touch the next problem.
- Can you rewrite those fractions? (Signal.) *Yes.*
- How do you know? (Signal.) *The wholes are the same.*
- What will you write on the bottom? (Signal.) *4.*
- What will you write on the top? (Signal.) *5 plus 2.*
- Rewrite the fractions. ✔

e. The wholes are the same, so you can make a picture. How many parts in each whole? (Signal.) *4.*
- Make the lines for the parts in each whole.

- You are going to show that you use 5 plus 2 parts. How many parts will you shade? (Signal.) *5.*
- How many parts will you dot? (Signal.) *2.*
f. Make the picture. Then work the rest of the problems in Part 3. You have 4 minutes.
- (Observe students and give feedback.)

EXERCISE 4

Numbers as Fractions

a. I'll say some numbers. You tell how to write each number as a fraction.
- How would you write 10 as a fraction? (Signal.) *10 over 1.*
- How would you write 2 as a fraction? (Signal.) *2 over 1.*
b. Touch the first problem in Part 4.
- You have to write each number as a fraction.
- How would you write the first number as a fraction? (Signal.) *6 over 1.*
- Touch the next problem.
- How would you write that number as a fraction? (Signal.) *5 over 1.*
c. Write each number in Part 4 as a fraction. You have 1 minute.
- (Observe students and give feedback.)

EXERCISE 5

Workcheck

a. We're going to check the answers. Exchange workbooks, and get ready to check the answers. (Pause.)
- Put an **X** next to each problem that the person misses.
- (Check and correct. See *Answer Key.*)
- Return the workbooks.
b. Now we're going to figure out the number of points you've earned for this lesson.
- (Point to the posted information.)

Worksheet Items	Errors	Points
	0–2	10
	3	7
	4	5
	5	3
	6	1
	7 or more	0

- Count the number of items you got wrong. Figure out the number of points you earned and write the number in the "Items" box.
- (Observe students and give feedback.)
c. (Tell the group how many points they earned for the lesson.) Write that number in the "Hard Work" box; then figure out the total for today's lesson.
d. Turn to the Point Summary Charts. Write the points in the box for Lesson 20. ✔
e. Total your points for Lessons 16 through 20 and write the total number on the chart.
- (Observe students and give feedback.)
f. Everybody, find the Five-Lesson Point Graph. ✔
- (Help the students plot their five-lesson scores on the graph.)

EXERCISE 1

Addition/Subtraction

a. Turn to Lesson 21 in your workbook.
- Touch the first problem in Part 1.
- You're going to write the fraction for that picture and use a plus sign.
- Tell me how many parts are in each whole. Get ready. (Signal.) *4.*
- Where do you write the 4? (Signal.) *On the bottom.*
- Write it. ✔
- Where will you write the number for the parts that are used? (Signal.) *On the top.*
- Tell me how many parts are shaded. Get ready. (Signal.) *3.*
- Write it. Then write the plus sign. ✔
- Tell me how many parts are dotted. Get ready. (Signal.) *2.*
- Write it. ✔

b. Now you have to rewrite the fraction. How much does 3 plus 2 equal? (Signal.) *5.*
- Tell me the complete fraction you will write in the box. (Signal.) *5 fourths.*
- Write it. ✔

c. Work the rest of the problems in Part 1 the same way. You have 3 minutes.
- (Observe students and give feedback.)

EXERCISE 2

Addition/Subtraction

a. Touch the first problem in Part 2.
- You're going to rewrite some of these fractions and then draw the picture.
- When can you rewrite fractions? (Signal.) *When the wholes are the same.*

b. Touch the first problem.
- Can you rewrite the fractions in that problem? (Signal.) *Yes.*
- How do you know? (Signal.) *The wholes are the same.*
- What will you write on the bottom? (Signal.) *3.*

- What will you write on the top? (Signal.) *2 plus 2.*
- Rewrite the fractions. ✔

c. The wholes are the same, so you can make a picture. How many parts in each whole? (Signal.) *3.*
- Make the lines for the parts in each whole. ✔
- Now show how many parts you use. Shade 2 parts. Then make dots for 2 more parts. ✔

d. Touch the next problem.
- Can you rewrite those fractions? (Signal.) *Yes.*
- How do you know? (Signal.) *The wholes are the same.*
- What will you write on the bottom? (Signal.) *4.*
- What will you write on the top? (Signal.) *3 plus 2.*
- Rewrite the fractions. ✔

e. The wholes are the same, so you can make a picture. How many parts in each whole? (Signal.) *4.*
- Make the lines for the parts in each whole.
- You are going to show that you use 3 plus 2 parts. How many parts will you shade? (Signal.) *3.*
- How many parts will you dot? (Signal.) *2.*

f. Make the picture. Then work the rest of the problems in Part 2 in the same way. You have 4 minutes.
- (Observe students and give feedback.)

EXERCISE 3

Numbers as Fractions

a. Touch the first problem in Part 3.
- You have to write how many wholes each fraction equals.
- Do the problems in Part 3. You have 1 minute.
- (Observe students and give feedback.)

b (After 1 minute, say:) In Part 4 there are some numbers. You have to write the fraction that each number equals.

- Touch the first number.
- How would you write that number as a fraction? (Signal.) *6 over 1.*
- Touch the next number.
- How would you write that number as a fraction? (Signal.) *12 over 1.*
- Do the problems in Part 4. Write the fraction for each number. You have 1 minute.
- (Observe students and give feedback.)

c. (After 1 minute, say:) Look at the problems in Part 5. For some problems you have to write the fraction for the number. For other problems you have to write the number for the fraction.
- Do the problems in Part 5. You have 2 minutes.
- (Observe students and give feedback.)

EXERCISE 4
Workcheck

a. We're going to check the answers. Exchange workbooks, and get ready to check the answers. (Pause.)
- Put an **X** next to each problem that the person misses.
- (Check and correct. See *Answer Key.*)
- Return the workbooks.

b. Now we're going to figure out the number of points you've earned for this lesson.
- (Point to the posted information.)

Worksheet Items	Errors	Points
	0–2	10
	3	7
	4	5
	5	3
	6	1
	7 or more	0

- Count the number of items you got wrong. Figure out the number of points you earned and write the number in the "Items" box.
- (Observe students and give feedback.)

c. (Tell the group how many points they earned for the lesson.) Write that number in the "Hard Work" box; then figure out the total for today's lesson.

d. Turn to the Point Summary Charts. Write the points in the box for Lesson 21. ✔

EXERCISE 1

More, Less, Equal to 1

a. Turn to Lesson 22 in your workbook.
- Touch the first problem in Part 1.
- Does that fraction equal 1? (Signal.) *No.*
- How do you know? (Signal.) *You don't use the same number of parts that are in each whole.*
- Tell me how many parts are in each whole. Get ready. (Signal.) *7.*
- Do you use more than 7 parts or less than 7 parts? (Signal.) *More.*
- So is that fraction more or less than 1? (Signal.) *More.*
- Circle the word **more.**

b. Work the rest of the problems in Part 1 in the same way. You have 2 minutes.
- (Observe students and give feedback.)

EXERCISE 2

Addition/Subtraction

a. When can you rewrite fractions? (Signal.) *When the wholes are the same.*
- Look at Part 2.
- You're going to rewrite some of these fractions and then draw the picture.

b. Touch the first problem.
- Can you rewrite the fractions in that problem? (Signal.) *No.*
- How do you know? (Signal.) *The wholes are not the same.*
- You can't rewrite them so you can't make a picture. You don't know whether to make 4 parts in each whole or 2 parts in each whole. So you can't make a picture. You don't do anything to that problem.

c. Touch the next problem.
- Can you rewrite those fractions? (Signal.) *Yes.*
- How do you know? (Signal.) *The wholes are the same.*
- When you rewrite those fractions, what will you write on the bottom? (Signal.) *3.*

- What will you write on the top? (Signal.) *3 plus 1.*
- Rewrite the fractions. ✔

d. Now draw the picture.
- First make the parts in each whole. (Pause.)
- Now shade the first parts you use. (Pause.)
- Dot the other parts you use. ✔

e. Touch the next problem.
- Can you rewrite those fractions? (Signal.) *Yes.*
- How do you know? (Signal.) *The wholes are the same.*
- Rewrite the fractions. ✔
- Now draw the picture. Remember to shade the first parts you use and dot the other parts you use. ✔

f. Work the rest of the problems in Part 2. Remember, if you can't rewrite the fractions, you can't make a picture. Just skip the problem. You have 4 minutes.
- (Observe students and give feedback.)

EXERCISE 3

Numbers as Fractions

a. In Part 3, you have to write how many wholes each fraction equals.
- Do the problems in Part 3.
- (Observe students and give feedback.)

b. (After the students have finished, say:) In Part 4 there are some numbers. You have to write the fraction that each number equals.
- Touch the first number.
- How would you write that number as a fraction? (Signal.) *5 over 1.*
- Do the problems in Part 4. Write the fraction for each number.
- (Observe students and give feedback.)

c. (After the students have finished, say:) Look at the problems in Part 5. For some problems you have to write the fraction for the number. For other problems you have to write the number for the fraction.
- Do all the problems in Part 5. You have 2 minutes.
- (Observe students and give feedback.)

EXERCISE 4

Workcheck

a. We're going to check the answers. Exchange workbooks, and get ready to check the answers. (Pause.)
- Put an **X** next to each problem that the person misses.
- (Check and correct. See *Answer Key.*)
- Return the workbooks.

b. Now we're going to figure out the number of points you've earned for this lesson.
- (Point to the posted information.)

Worksheet Items	Errors	Points
	0–2	10
	3	7
	4	5
	5	3
	6	1
	7 or more	0

- Count the number of items you got wrong. Figure out the number of points you earned and write the number in the "Items" box.
- (Observe students and give feedback.)

c. (Tell the group how many points they earned for the lesson.) Write that number in the "Hard Work" box; then figure out the total for today's lesson.

d. Turn to the Point Summary Charts. Write the points in the box for Lesson 22. ✔

EXERCISE 1

Numbers as Fractions

a. Turn to Lesson 23. In Part 1, you have to write how many wholes each fraction equals.
 • Do the problems in Part 1.
 • (Observe students and give feedback.)
b. (After the students have finished, say:) In Part 2 there are some numbers. You have to write the fraction that each number equals.
 • Touch the first number.
 • How would you write that number as a fraction? (Signal.) *1 over 1.*
 • Do the problems in Part 2. Write the fraction for each number.
 • (Observe students and give feedback.)
c. (After the students have finished, say:) Look at the problems in Part 3. For some problems you have to write the fraction for the number. For other problems you have to write the number for the fraction.
 • Do the problems in Part 3. You have 2 minutes.
 • (Observe students and give feedback.)

EXERCISE 2

Addition/Subtraction

a. When can you rewrite fractions that are added or subtracted? (Signal.) *When the wholes are the same.*
 • Look at Part 4. You're going to rewrite some of these fractions and then draw the picture.
b. Touch the first problem.
 • Can you rewrite those fractions? (Signal.) *No.*
 • How do you know? (Signal.) *The wholes are not the same.*
 • You can't rewrite them so you can't make a picture. You don't know whether to make 2 parts in each whole or 3 parts in each whole. So you can't make a picture. You don't do anything to that problem.
c. Touch the next problem.

• Can you rewrite those fractions? (Signal.) *Yes.*
 • How do you know? (Signal.) *The wholes are the same.*
 • Rewrite those fractions. ✔
d. Now draw the picture. Remember to shade the first parts you use and dot the other parts you use. ✔
e. Work the rest of the problems in Part 4. Remember, if you can't rewrite the fractions, you can't make a picture. Just skip the problem. You have 3 minutes.
 • (Observe students and give feedback.)

EXERCISE 3

Multiplication

a. (Write on the board:)
★

$$\frac{4}{5} \times \frac{3}{4} = \boxed{\frac{}{}}$$

• What does the sign say to do? (Signal.) *Multiply.*
b. Here's how we multiply fractions.
 • We multiply top times the top and bottom times the bottom. How do we multiply fractions? (Signal.) *Top times the top and bottom times the bottom.*
 • (Repeat until firm.)
c. Read the top. (Touch each part as the students read.) *4 times 3.*
 • Tell me what the top equals. Get ready. (Signal.) *12.*
 • The top equals 12. We write it on the top. Where do we write the 12? (Signal.) *On the top.*
 • (Write to show:)

$$\frac{4}{5} \times \frac{3}{4} = \boxed{\frac{12}{}}$$

d. Read the bottom. (Touch each part as the students read.) *5 times 4.*
 • Tell me what the bottom equals. Get ready. (Signal.) *20.*

- Where do we write the 20? (Signal.) *On the bottom.*
- (Write to show:)

$$\frac{4}{5} \times \frac{3}{4} = \boxed{\frac{12}{20}}$$

- 4 fifths times 3 fourths equals 12 twentieths. It sounds funny, but that's the answer.

e. (Write on the board:)

$$\frac{3}{2} \times \frac{6}{5} = \boxed{\frac{}{}}$$

- What does the sign say to do? (Signal.) *Multiply.*
- How do we multiply fractions? (Signal.) *Top times the top and bottom times the bottom.*

f. Read the top. (Signal.) *3 times 6.*
- Tell me what the top equals. Get ready. (Signal.) *18.*
- Where do I write the 18? (Signal.) *On the top.*
- (Write to show:)

$$\frac{3}{2} \times \frac{6}{5} = \boxed{\frac{18}{}}$$

g. Read the bottom. *2 times 5.*
- Tell me what the bottom equals. Get ready. (Signal.) *10.*
- Where do I write the ten? (Signal.) *On the bottom.*
- (Write to show:)

$$\frac{3}{2} \times \frac{6}{5} = \boxed{\frac{18}{10}}$$

- 3 halves times 6 fifths.
- Read the answer. (Signal.) *18 tenths.*

h. Turn to Part 5 in your workbook. Touch the first problem.
- What does the sign say to do? (Signal.) *Multiply.*
- How do you multiply fractions? (Signal.) *Top times the top and bottom times the bottom.*
- Touch the top.

- Figure out the answer when you multiply. (Pause.)
- Tell me what the top equals. Get ready. (Signal.) *6.*
- Write it in the answer box. ✔
- Touch the bottom.
- Figure out the answer when you multiply. (Pause.)
- What does the bottom equal? (Signal.) *12.*
- Write it in the answer box. ✔
- 3 sixths times 2 halves. What's the answer? (Signal.) *6 twelfths.*
- Right, 6 twelfths.

i. Touch the next problem.
- What does the sign say to do? (Signal.) *Multiply.*
- How do you multiply fractions? (Signal.) *Top times the top and bottom times the bottom.*
- Touch the top.
- Figure out the answer when you multiply. (Pause.)
- What does the top equal? (Signal.) *18.*
- Write it in the answer box. ✔
- Touch the bottom.
- Figure out the answer when you multiply.
- What does the bottom equal? (Signal.) *28.*
- Write it in the answer box. ✔
- 3 fourths times 6 sevenths. What's the answer? (Signal.) *18/28ths.*
- Right, 18/28ths.

j. Do the rest of the problems in Part 5. Remember, you multiply top times the top and bottom times the bottom. You have 4 minutes.
- (Observe students and give feedback.)

EXERCISE 4
Workcheck

a. We're going to check the answers. Exchange workbooks, and get ready to check the answers. (Pause.)
- Put an **X** next to each problem that the person misses.
- (Check and correct. See **Answer Key.**)
- Return the workbooks.

b. Now we're going to figure out the number of points you've earned for this lesson.

- (Point to the posted information.)

Worksheet Items	Errors	Points
	0–2	10
	3	7
	4	5
	5	3
	6	1
	7 or more	0

- Count the number of items you got wrong. Figure out the number of points you earned and write the number in the "Items" box.
- (Observe students and give feedback.)

c. (Tell the group how many points they earned for the lesson.) Write that number in the "Hard Work" box; then figure out the total for today's lesson.
d. Turn to the Point Summary Charts. Write the points in the box for Lesson 23. ✔

Lesson 24

Skipping Note: Check the students' errors from Lesson 23. If no more than 1 fourth of the students made more than 4 errors, skip this lesson and proceed with Lesson 25.

EXERCISE 1

Addition/Subtraction

a. Turn to Lesson 24 in your workbook
- Touch the first problem in Part 1.
- Can you rewrite the fractions in that problem? (Signal.) *Yes.*
- How do you know? (Signal.) *The wholes are the same.*
- When you rewrite those fractions, what will you write on the bottom? (Signal.) *4.*
- What will you write on the top? (Signal.) *2 plus 7.*
- Rewrite the fractions. ✔
- Now you have to write the fraction in the box. How much does 2 plus 7 equal? (Signal.) *9.*
- Tell me the complete fraction you will write in the box. (Signal.) *9 fourths.*
- Write it. ✔

b. Touch the next problem.
- Can you rewrite those fractions? (Signal.) *No.*
- How do you know? (Signal.) *The wholes aren't the same.*
- You can't do anything to that problem. You just skip it.

c. Work the rest of the problems in Part 1. Remember, if you can't rewrite the fractions, skip the problem. You have 3 minutes.
- (Observe students and give feedback.)

EXERCISE 2

Addition/Subtraction

a. When can you rewrite fractions that you add or subtract? (Signal.) *When the wholes are the same.*
- Look at Part 2.

- You're going to rewrite some of these fractions and then draw the picture.
b. Touch the first problem.
- Can you rewrite those fractions? (Signal.) *No.*
- How do you know? (Signal.) *The wholes aren't the same.*
- You can't rewrite them so you can't make a picture. You don't know whether to make 3 parts in each whole or 4 parts in each whole. So you can't make a picture. You don't do anything to that problem.
c. Touch the next problem.
- Can you rewrite those fractions? (Signal.) *Yes.*
- How do you know? (Signal.) *The wholes are the same.*
- Rewrite those fractions. ✔
d. Now draw the picture. Remember to shade the first parts you use and dot the other parts you use. ✔
e. Work the rest of the problems in Part 2. Remember, if you can't rewrite the fractions, you can't make a picture. Just skip the problem. You have 3 minutes.
- (Observe students and give feedback.)

EXERCISE 3

Multiplication

a. (Write on the board:)

$$\frac{3}{5} \times \frac{2}{3} = \boxed{\frac{}{}}$$

- What does the sign say to do? (Signal.) *Multiply.*
b. How do we multiply fractions? (Signal.) *Top times the top and bottom times the bottom.*
- (Repeat until firm.)
c. Read the top. (Touch each part as the students read.) *3 times 2.*
- Tell me what the top equals. Get ready. (Signal.) *6.*
- The top equals 6. Where do we write the 6? (Signal.) *On the top.*

- (Write to show:)

$$\frac{3}{5} \times \frac{2}{3} = \boxed{6}$$

d. Read the bottom. (Touch each part as the students read.) *5 times 3.*
- Tell me what the bottom equals. Get ready. (Signal.) *15.*
- Where do we write the fifteen? (Signal.) *On the bottom.*
- (Write to show:)

$$\frac{3}{5} \times \frac{2}{3} = \boxed{\frac{6}{15}}$$

- 3 fifths times 2 thirds. What's the answer? (Signal.) *6/15ths.*
- It sounds funny, but that's the right answer.
e. Turn to Part 3 in your workbook.
- Touch the first problem.
- What does the sign say to do? (Signal.) *Multiply.*
- How do you multiply fractions? (Signal.) *Top times the top and bottom times the bottom.*
- Touch the top.
- Figure out the answer when you multiply. (Pause.)
- What does the top equal? (Signal.) *7.*
- Write it in the answer box. ✔
- Touch the bottom.
- Figure out the answer when you multiply. (Pause.)
- What does the bottom equal? (Signal.) *20.*
- Write it in the answer box. ✔
- 1 fifth times 7 fourths. What's the answer? (Signal.) *7/20ths.*
- Right, 7/20ths.
f. Touch the next problem.
- What does the sign say to do? (Signal.) *Multiply.*
- How do you multiply fractions? (Signal.) *Top times the top and bottom times the bottom.*
- Touch the top.
- Figure out the answer when you multiply. (Pause.)
- What does the top equal? (Signal.) *6.*

- Write it in the answer box. ✔
- Touch the bottom.
- Figure out the answer when you multiply. (Pause.)
- What does the bottom equal? (Signal.) *12.*
- Write it in the answer box. ✔
- 3 halves times 2 sixths. What's the answer? (Signal.) *6 twelfths.*
- Right, 6 twelfths.
g. Do the rest of the problems in Part 3. You have 4 minutes.
- (Observe students and give feedback.)

EXERCISE 4

Workcheck

a. We're going to check the answers. Exchange workbooks, and get ready to check the answers. (Pause.)
- Put an **X** next to each problem that the person misses.
- (Check and correct. See **Answer Key.**)
- Return the workbooks.
b. Now we're going to figure out the number of points you've earned for this lesson.
- (Point to the posted information.)

Worksheet Items	Errors	Points
	0–2	10
	3	7
	4	5
	5	3
	6	1
	7 or more	0

- Count the number of items you got wrong. Figure out the number of points you earned and write the number in the "Items" box.
- (Observe students and give feedback.)
c. (Tell the group how many points they earned for the lesson.) Write that number in the "Hard Work" box; then figure out the total for today's lesson.
d. Turn to the Point Summary Charts. Write the points in the box for Lesson 24. ✔

EXERCISE 1

Numbers as Fractions

a. Turn to Lesson 25.
- Look at the problems in Part 1.
- Some of the fractions are equal to 1. Some of the fractions are equal to other numbers. The first fraction is 7 over 1. How many wholes does that equal? (Signal.) *7.*

b. The next fraction is 7 over 7. How many wholes does that equal? (Signal.) *1.*

c. Do all the problems in Part 1. You have 2 minutes.
- (Observe students and give feedback.)

d. (After 2 minutes, say:) Look at the problems in Part 2. There are some numbers and some fractions. Write a fraction for each number and write a number for each fraction.
- Do the problems in Part 2. You have 1 minute.
- (Observe students and give feedback.)

EXERCISE 2

Multiplication

a. Touch the first problem in Part 3.
- What does the sign say to do? (Signal.) *Multiply.*
- How do you multiply fractions? (Signal.) *Top times the top and bottom times the bottom.*
- Touch the top.
- Tell me what the top equals. Get ready. (Signal.) *8.*
- Write it in the answer box. ✔
- Touch the bottom.
- Tell me what the bottom equals. Get ready. (Signal.) *9.*
- Write it in the answer box. ✔
- 2 thirds times 4 thirds. What's the answer? (Signal.) *8 ninths.*
- Right, 8 ninths. It sounds funny, but it's right.

b. Touch the next problem.
- What does the sign say to do? (Signal.) *Multiply.*

- How do you multiply fractions? (Signal.) *Top times the top and bottom times the bottom.*
- Touch the top.
- Tell me what the top equals. Get ready. (Signal.) *15.*
- Write it in the answer box. ✔
- Touch the bottom.
- Tell me what the bottom equals. Get ready. (Signal.) *20.*
- Write it in the answer box. ✔
- 3 fourths times 5 fifths. What's the answer? (Signal.) *15/20ths.*
- Right, 15/20ths.

c. Do the rest of the problems in Part 3. You have 4 minutes.
- (Observe students and give feedback.)

EXERCISE 3

Addition/Subtraction

a. Touch the first problem in Part 4.
- Can you rewrite the fractions in that problem? (Signal.) *Yes.*
- How do you know? (Signal.) *The wholes are the same.*
- When you rewrite those fractions, what will you write on the bottom? (Signal.) *5.*
- What will you write on the top? (Signal.) *7 plus 3.*
- Rewrite the fractions. ✔
- Now you have to write the fraction in the box. How much does 7 plus 3 equal? (Signal.) *10.*
- Tell me the complete fraction you will write in the box. (Signal.) *10 fifths.*
- Write it. ✔

b. Touch the next problem.
- Can you rewrite those fractions? (Signal.) *No.*
- How do you know? (Signal.) *The wholes aren't the same.*
- You can't do anything to that problem. You just skip it.

c. Work the rest of the problems in Part 4. Remember, if you can't rewrite the fractions, skip the problem. You have 3 minutes.
- (Observe students and give feedback.)

EXERCISE 4

Workcheck

a. We're going to check the answers. Exchange workbooks, and get ready to check the answers. (Pause.)
- Put an **X** next to each problem that the person misses.
- (Check and correct. See **Answer Key.**)
- Return the workbooks.

b. Now we're going to figure out the number of points you've earned for this lesson.
- (Point to the posted information.)

Worksheet Items	Errors	Points
	0–2	10
	3	7
	4	5
	5	3
	6	1
	7 or more	0

- Count the number of items you got wrong. Figure out the number of points you earned and write the number in the "Items" box.
- (Observe students and give feedback.)

c. (Tell the group how many points they earned for the lesson.) Write that number in the "Hard Work" box; then figure out the total for today's lesson.

d. Turn to the Point Summary Charts. Write the points in the box for Lesson 25. ✔

e. Total your points for Lessons 21 through 25 and write the total number on the chart.
- (Observe students and give feedback.)

f. Everybody, find the Five-Lesson Point Graph. ✔
- (Help the students plot their five-lesson scores on the graph.)

Skipping Note: Check the students' errors from Lesson 25. If no more than 1 fourth of the students made more than 4 errors, skip this lesson and proceed with Lesson 27.

EXERCISE 1

Numbers as Fractions

a. Open your workbooks to Lesson 26. Look at the problems in Part 1.
- Some of the fractions are equal to 1. Some of the fractions are equal to other numbers. The first fraction is 3 over 1. How many wholes does that equal? (Signal.) *3.*

b. The next fraction is 3 over 3. How many wholes does that equal? (Signal.) *1.*
- Do all the problems in Part 1. You have 1 minute.

c. (After 1 minute, say:) In the next part you have to write a fraction for each number. The first number is 4. How do you write 4 as a fraction? (Signal.) *4 over 1.*
- The next number is 17. How do you write 17 as a fraction? (Signal.) *17 over 1.*
- Write the fraction for each number in Part 2. You have 1 minute.

d. (After 1 minute, say:) Look at the problems in Part 3. There are some numbers and some fractions. Write a fraction for each number and write a number for each fraction. Do all of the problems in Part 3. You have 2 minutes.
- (Observe students and give feedback.)

EXERCISE 2

Addition/Subtraction

a. Touch the first problem in Part 4.
- Can you rewrite the fractions in that problem? (Signal.) *Yes.*
- Rewrite the fractions. ✔
- Now you have to write the fraction on the next line. How much does 4 plus 3 equal? (Signal.) *7.*

- Tell me the complete fraction you will write on the line. (Signal.) *7 fifths.*
- Write it. ✔

b. Work the rest of the problems in Part 4. Write the answer on the line. Remember, if you can't rewrite the fractions, skip the problem. You have 2 minutes.
- (Observe students and give feedback.)

EXERCISE 3

Multiplication

a. (Write on the board:)

★
$$3 \times \frac{4}{5} = \underline{} \qquad \frac{1 \times 5}{3} = \underline{}$$
$$\frac{3 \times 6}{4} = \underline{}$$

b. In each of these problems, one of the numbers is not written as a fraction.
- (Point to $3 \times \frac{4}{5}$.)
- In this problem, which number is not written as a fraction? (Signal.) *3.*
- (Point to $\frac{1 \times 5}{3}$.)
- In this problem, which number is not written as a fraction? (Signal.) *5.*
- (Point to $\frac{3 \times 6}{4}$.)
- In this problem, which number is not written as a fraction? (Signal.) *6.*

c. (Point to the 3 in $3 \times \frac{4}{5}$.)
- Let's change the number into a fraction so that we can multiply. Tell me how to write this number as a fraction. (Signal.) *3 over 1.*
- (Change 3 to $\frac{3}{1}$.)
- Now we can multiply. What's the answer for the top? (Signal.) *12.*

- (Write to show:)

$$\frac{3}{1} \times \frac{4}{5} = \frac{12}{}$$

- What's the answer for the bottom? (Signal.) *5.*
- (Write to show:)

$$\frac{3}{1} \times \frac{4}{5} = \frac{12}{5}$$

- What's the answer to the problem? (Signal.) *12 fifths.*

d. (Point to the 5 in $\frac{1 \times 5}{3}$.)

- Tell me how to write this number as a fraction. (Signal.) *5 over 1.*
- (Change 5 to $\frac{5}{1}$.)
- Now we can multiply. What's the answer for the top? (Signal.) *5.*
- (Write to show:)

$$\frac{1}{3} \times \frac{5}{1} = \frac{5}{}$$

- What's the answer for the bottom? (Signal.) *3.*
- (Write on the board:)

$$\frac{1}{3} \times \frac{5}{1} = \frac{5}{3}$$

- What's the answer to the problem? (Signal.) *5 thirds.*

e. (Point to the 6 in $\frac{3 \times 6}{4}$.)

- Tell me how to write this number as a fraction. (Signal.) *6 over 1.*
- (Change 6 to $\frac{6}{1}$.)
- Now we can multiply. What's the answer for the top? (Signal.) *18.*

- (Write on the board:)

$$\frac{3}{4} \times \frac{6}{1} = \frac{18}{}$$

- What's the answer for the bottom? (Signal.) *4.*
- (Write on the board:)

$$\frac{3}{4} \times \frac{6}{1} = \frac{18}{4}$$

- What's the answer to the problem? (Signal.) *18 fourths.*

f. Look at the problems in Part 5. Before you can multiply some of these problems, you have to change a number into a fraction.
- Work all of the problems in Part 5. You have 4 minutes.
- (Observe students and give feedback.)

EXERCISE 4

More, Less, Equal to 1

a. Look at the problems in Part 6. You have to figure out whether the fraction is more than 1, equal to 1, or less than 1.

b. Do the problems in Part 6. You have 2 minutes.
- (Observe students and give feedback.)

EXERCISE 5

Workcheck

a. We're going to check the answers. Exchange workbooks, and get ready to check the answers. (Pause.)
- Put an **X** next to each problem that the person misses.
- (Check and correct. See **Answer Key.**)
- Return the workbooks.

b. Now we're going to figure out the number of points you've earned for this lesson.

- (Point to the posted information.)

Worksheet Items	Errors	Points
	0–2	10
	3	7
	4	5
	5	3
	6	1
	7 or more	0

- Count the number of items you got wrong. Figure out the number of points you earned and write the number in the "Items" box.
- (Observe students and give feedback.)

c. (Tell the group how many points they earned for the lesson.) Write that number in the "Hard Work" box; then figure out the total for today's lesson.
d. Turn to the Point Summary Charts. Write the points in the box for Lesson 26. ✔

EXERCISE 1

Numbers as Fractions

a. Turn to Lesson 27.
- Look at the problems in Part 1.
- Some of the fractions are equal to 1. Some of the fractions are equal to other numbers. The first fraction is 4 over 4.
- Do all the problems in Part 1. You have 1 minute.
- (Observe students and give feedback.)

b. (After the students have finished, say:) In Part 2 you have to write a fraction for each number. Write the fraction for each number in Part 2.

c. (After the students have finished, say:) Look at the problems in Part 3.
- Write a fraction for each number and write a number for each fraction. You have 1 minute.
- (Observe students and give feedback.)

EXERCISE 2

Multiplication

a. (Write on the board:)

$$\frac{3 \times 5}{7} = — \qquad \frac{2 \times 8}{3} = —$$

b. (Point to the 3 in $\frac{3 \times 5}{7}$.)

- Let's change the number into a fraction so that we can multiply. Tell me how to write this number as a fraction. (Signal.) *3 over 1.*
- (Change 3 to $\frac{3}{1}$.)
- Now we can multiply. What's the answer for the top? (Signal.) *15.*
- (Write to show:)

$$\frac{3}{1} \times \frac{5}{7} = \frac{15}{}$$

- What's the answer for the bottom? (Signal.) *7.*

- (Write to show:)

$$\frac{3}{1} \times \frac{5}{7} = \frac{15}{7}$$

- What's the answer to the problem? (Signal.) *15 sevenths.*

c. (Point to the 8 in $\frac{2 \times 8}{3}$.)

- Tell me how to write this number as a fraction. (Signal.) *8 over 1.*
- (Change 8 to $\frac{8}{1}$.)
- Now we can multiply. What's the answer for the top? (Signal.) *16.*
- (Write to show:)

$$\frac{2}{3} \times \frac{8}{1} = \frac{16}{}$$

- What's the answer for the bottom? (Signal.) *3.*
- (Write to show:)

$$\frac{2}{3} \times \frac{8}{1} = \frac{16}{3}$$

d. Find Part 4 on your worksheet. Before you can multiply some of these problems, you have to change a number into a fraction.
- Work all of the problems in Part 4. You have 3 minutes.
- (Observe students and give feedback.)

EXERCISE 3

Addition/Subtraction

a. Touch the first problem in Part 5.
- Can you rewrite the fractions in that problem? (Signal.) *Yes.*
- Rewrite the fractions. ✔
- Now you have to write the fraction on the next line. How much does 2 plus 7 equal? (Signal.) *9.*
- Tell me the complete fraction you will write in the box. (Signal.) *9 sevenths.*
- Write it. ✔

b. Work the rest of the problems in Part 5. Remember, if you can't rewrite the fractions, skip the problem. You have 3 minutes.
- (Observe students and give feedback.)

EXERCISE 4
Addition/Subtraction

a. When can you rewrite fractions? (Signal.) *When the wholes are the same.*
- You are going to work the problems in Part 6 without rewriting them.

b. Touch the first problem.
- Can you rewrite the fractions in that problem? (Signal.) *Yes.*
- What do you write on the bottom? (Signal.) *5.*
- Write it. ✔
- Read what you would write for the top. (Signal.) *7 plus 3.*
- What does that equal? (Signal.) *10.*
- Write that for the top. ✔
- What's the answer to the problem? (Signal.) *10 fifths.*

c. Work the next problem on your own. ✔
- What's the answer? (Signal.) *9 fourths*

d. Work the rest of the problems in Part 6. You have 3 minutes.
- (Observe students and give feedback.)

EXERCISE 5
Workcheck

a. We're going to check the answers. Exchange workbooks, and get ready to check the answers. (Pause.)
- Put an **X** next to each problem that the person misses.
- (Check and correct. See *Answer Key.*)
- Return the workbooks.

b. Now we're going to figure out the number of points you've earned for this lesson.
- (Point to the posted information.)

Worksheet Items	Errors	Points
	0–2	10
	3	7
	4	5
	5	3
	6	1
	7 or more	0

- Count the number of items you got wrong. Figure out the number of points you earned and write the number in the "Items" box.
- (Observe students and give feedback.)

c. (Tell the group how many points they earned for the lesson.) Write that number in the "Hard Work" box; then figure out the total for today's lesson.

d. Turn to the Point Summary Charts. Write the points in the box for Lesson 27. ✔

Lesson 28

EXERCISE 1

Addition/Subtraction

a. Turn to Lesson 28.
- Find Part 1. Touch the first problem.
- Can you rewrite the fractions in that problem? (Signal.) *Yes.*
- How do you know? (Signal.) *The wholes are the same.*
- When you rewrite those fractions, what will you write on the bottom? (Signal.) *2.*
- What will you write on the top? (Signal.) *2 plus 7.*
- Rewrite the fractions. ✔
- Now you have to write the fraction on the next line. How much does 2 plus 7 equal? (Signal.) *9.*
- Tell me the complete fraction you will write on the next line. (Signal.) *9 halves.*
- Write it. ✔

b. Touch the next problem.
- Can you rewrite those fractions? (Signal.) *No.*
- How do you know? (Signal.) *The wholes aren't the same.*
- You can't do anything to that problem. You just skip it.

c. Work the rest of the problems in Part 1. Remember, if you can't rewrite the fractions, skip that problem. You have 3 minutes.
- (Observe students and give feedback.)

EXERCISE 2

Addition/Subtraction

a. When can you rewrite fractions that you add or subtract? (Signal.) *When the wholes are the same.*
- You're going to work the problems in Part 2 without rewriting them. You won't be able to work some of the problems, so you'll just skip them.

b. Touch the first problem.
- Can you rewrite those fractions? (Signal.) *No.*
- So skip that problem.

c. Touch the next problem.
- Can you rewrite those fractions? (Signal.) *Yes.*
- Work that problem. (Pause.)
- What's the answer? (Signal.) *6 fifths.*

d. Work the rest of the problems in Part 2. Remember to skip the problem if you can't rewrite the fractions. You have 4 minutes.
- (Observe students and give feedback.)

EXERCISE 3

Multiplication

a. (Write on the board:)

$$5 \times \frac{3}{7} = \text{—}$$

b. (Point to the 5 in $5 \times \frac{3}{7}$.)
- Let's change the number into a fraction so that we can multiply. Tell me how to write this number as a fraction. (Signal.) *5 over 1.*
- (Change 5 to $\frac{5}{1}$.)
- Now we can multiply. What's the answer for the top? (Signal.) *15.*
- (Write on the board:)

$$\frac{5}{1} \times \frac{3}{7} = \frac{15}{}$$

- What's the answer for the bottom? (Signal.) *7.*
- (Write on the board:)

$$\frac{5}{1} \times \frac{3}{7} = \frac{15}{7}$$

- What's the answer to the problem? (Signal.) *15 sevenths.*

c. Look at the problems in Part 3.
- In the first problem, do you have to write any numbers as fractions before you multiply? (Signal.) *Yes.*
- Tell me what you will write for that number. (Signal.) *3 over 1.*

d. Work all of the problems in Part 3. In some problem you will have to change numbers into fractions before you multiply. You have 4 minutes.

• (Observe students and give feedback.)

EXERCISE 4

Workcheck

a. We're going to check the answers. Exchange workbooks, and get ready to check the answers. (Pause.)

• Put an **X** next to each problem that the person misses.

• (Check and correct. See *Answer Key.*)

• Return the workbooks.

b. Now we're going to figure out the number of points you've earned for this lesson.

• (Point to the posted information.)

Worksheet Items	Errors	Points
	0–2	10
	3	7
	4	5
	5	3
	6	1
	7 or more	0

• Count the number of items you got wrong. Figure out the number of points you earned and write the number in the "Items" box.

• (Observe students and give feedback.)

c. (Tell the group how many points they earned for the lesson.) Write that number in the "Hard Work" box; then figure out the total for today's lesson.

d. Turn to the Point Summary Charts. Write the points in the box for Lesson 28. ✔

Lesson 29

EXERCISE 1

Numbers as Fractions

a. Turn to Lesson 29.
- Look at the problems in Part 1.
- Write a fraction for each number and write a number for each fraction.

b. Do all the problems in Part 1. You have 1 minute.
- (Observe students and give feedback.)

EXERCISE 2

Addition/Subtraction

a. Find Part 2. Touch the first problem.
- Can you rewrite the fractions in that problem? (Signal.) *Yes.*
- How do you know? (Signal.) *The wholes are the same.*
- When you rewrite those fractions, what will you write on the bottom? (Signal.) *4.*
- What will you write on the top? (Signal.) *5 plus 2.*
- Rewrite the fractions. ✔
- Now you have to write the fraction on the next line. How much does 5 plus 2 equal? (Signal.) *7.*
- Tell me the complete fraction you will write on the next line. (Signal.) *7 fourths.*
- Write it. ✔

b. Touch the next problem.
- Can you rewrite those fractions? (Signal.) *No.*
- How do you know? (Signal.) *The wholes aren't the same.*
- You can't do anything to that problem. You just skip it.

c. Work the rest of the problems in Part 2. Remember, if you can't rewrite the fractions, skip that problem. You have 2 minutes.
- (Observe students and give feedback.)

EXERCISE 3

Addition/Subtraction

a. When can you rewrite fractions that you add or subtract? (Signal.) *When the wholes are the same.*
- You are going to work the problems in Part 3 without rewriting them. You won't be able to work some of the problems, so you'll just skip them.

b. Touch the first problem.
- Can you rewrite those fractions? (Signal.) *No.*
- So skip that problem.

c. Touch the next problem.
- Can you rewrite those fractions? (Signal.) *Yes.*
- Work that problem. (Pause.)
- What's the answer? (Signal.) *7 tenths.*

d. Work the rest of the problems in Part 3. Remember to skip the problems if you can't rewrite the fractions. You have 3 minutes.
- (Observe students and give feedback.)

EXERCISE 4

Multiplication

a. Find Part 4 on your worksheet.
- In the first problem, do you have to write any numbers as fractions before you multiply? (Signal.) *Yes.*
- Tell me what you will write for that number. (Signal.) *3 over 1.*

b. Work all of the problems in Part 4. In some problems you will have to change numbers into fractions before you multiply. You have 3 minutes.
- (Observe students and give feedback.)

EXERCISE 5

Workcheck

a. We're going to check the answers. Exchange workbooks, and get ready to check the answers. (Pause.)

• Put an **X** next to each problem that the person misses.

• (Check and correct. See *Answer Key.*)

• Return the workbooks.

b. Now we're going to figure out the number of points you've earned for this lesson.

• (Point to the posted information.)

Worksheet Items	Errors	Points
	0–2	10
	3	7
	4	5
	5	3
	6	1
	7 or more	0

• Count the number of items you got wrong. Figure out the number of points you earned and write the number in the "Items" box.

• (Observe students and give feedback.)

c. (Tell the group how many points they earned for the lesson.) Write that number in the "Hard Work" box; then figure out the total for today's lesson.

d. Turn to the Point Summary Charts. Write the points in the box for Lesson 29. ✔

EXERCISE 1

Addition/Subtraction

a. When can you rewrite fractions that you add or subtract? (Signal.) *When the wholes are the same.*

b. Turn to Lesson 30. You're going to work the problems in Part 1 without rewriting them. You won't be able to work some of the problems, so you'll just skip them.

c. Touch the first problem.
- Can you rewrite those fractions? (Signal.) *No.*
- So skip that problem.

d. Touch the next problem.
- Can you rewrite those fractions? (Signal.) *Yes.*
- Work that problem. You have to write the line in the answer. (Pause.)
- What's the answer? (Signal.) *6 fifths.*

e. Work the rest of the problems in Part 1. Remember to skip the problems if you can't rewrite the fractions. Remember to write the line in the answer. You have 3 minutes.
- (Observe students and give feedback.)

EXERCISE 2

Multiplication

a. Look at the problems in Part 2 on your worksheet.
- In the first problem, do you have to write any numbers as fractions before you multiply? (Signal.) *Yes.*
- Tell me what you'll write for that number. (Signal.) *2 over 1.*

b. Work all of the problems in Part 2. In some problem you'll have to change numbers into fractions before you multiply. Remember the line in the answer. You have 3 minutes.
- (Observe students and give feedback.)

EXERCISE 3

Multiplication/Addition/ Subtraction

a. Look at the problems in Part 3. In some of these problems, you add or subtract. In some of the problems, you multiply.

b. When you add or subtract, you have to be able to rewrite the problem. When you multiply, you multiply top times the top and bottom times the bottom.

c. First I want you to tell me whether the problem is the kind you can rewrite to add or subtract or the kind you multiply top times the top and bottom times the bottom.
- Touch the first problem.
- Do you rewrite to add or subtract or do you multiply top times the top and bottom times the bottom? (Signal.) *Rewrite to add or subtract.*

d. Touch the next problem.
- Do you rewrite to add or subtract or do you multiply top times the top and bottom times the bottom? (Signal.) *Multiply top times the top and bottom times the bottom.*

e. Touch the next problem.
- Do you rewrite to add or subtract or do you multiply top times the top and bottom times the bottom? (Signal.) *Rewrite to add or subtract.*

f. Work all of the problems in Part 3. If the problem is the kind you can rewrite to add or subtract, work it the fast way. Remember to write the line in the answer. You have 4 minutes.
- (Observe students and give feedback.)

EXERCISE 4

More, Less, Equal to 1

a. Look at the problems in Part 4.
- You have to figure out whether the fraction is more than 1, equal to 1, or less than 1.

b. Do the problems in Part 4. You have 2 minutes.
- (Observe students and give feedback.)

EXERCISE 5

Workcheck

a. We're going to check the answers. Exchange workbooks, and get ready to check the answers. (Pause.)
- Put an **X** next to each problem that the person misses.
- (Check and correct. See *Answer Key.*)
- Return the workbooks.

b. Now we're going to figure out the number of points you've earned for this lesson.
- (Point to the posted information.)

Worksheet Items	Errors	Points
	0–2	10
	3	7
	4	5
	5	3
	6	1
	7 or more	0

- Count the number of items you got wrong. Figure out the number of points you earned and write the number in the "Items" box.
- (Observe students and give feedback.)

c. (Tell the group how many points they earned for the lesson.) Write that number in the "Hard Work" box; then figure out the total for today's lesson.

d. Turn to the Point Summary Charts. Write the points in the box for Lesson 30. ✔

e. Total your points for Lessons 26 through 30 and write the total number on the chart.
- (Observe students and give feedback.)

f. Everybody, find the Five-Lesson Point Graph. ✔
- (Help the students plot their five-lesson scores on the graph.)

EXERCISE 1

Multiplication/Addition/Subtraction

a. Turn to Lesson 31.
- Look at the problems in Part 1.
- In some of these problems, you add or subtract. In some of the problems, you multiply.

b. When you add or subtract, you have to be able to rewrite the problem. When you multiply, you multiply top times the top and bottom times the bottom.

c. First I want you to tell me whether the problem is the kind you can rewrite to add or subtract or the kind you multiply top times the top and bottom times the bottom.
- Touch the first problem.
- Do you rewrite to add or subtract or do you multiply top times the top and bottom times the bottom? (Signal.) *Rewrite to add or subtract.*

d. Touch the next problem.
- Do you rewrite to add or subtract or do you multiply top times the top and bottom times the bottom? (Signal.) *Rewrite to add or subtract.*

e. Touch the next problem.
- Do you rewrite to add or subtract or do you multiply top times the top and bottom times the bottom? (Signal.) *Multiply top times the top and bottom times the bottom.*

f. Work all of the problems in Part 1. If the problem is the kind you can rewrite to add or subtract, work it the fast way. Remember to write the line in the answer. You have 10 minutes.
- (Observe students and give feedback.)

EXERCISE 2

Workcheck

a. We're going to check the answers. Exchange workbooks, and get ready to check the answers. (Pause.)
- Put an **X** next to each problem that the person misses.
- (Check and correct. See *Answer Key*.)
- Return the workbooks.

b. Now we're going to figure out the number of points you've earned for this lesson.
- (Point to the posted information.)

Worksheet Items	Errors	Points
	0–2	10
	3	7
	4	5
	5	3
	6	1
	7 or more	0

- Count the number of items you got wrong. Figure out the number of points you earned and write the number in the "Items" box.
- (Observe students and give feedback.)

c. (Tell the group how many points they earned for the lesson.) Write that number in the "Hard Work" box; then figure out the total for today's lesson.

d. Turn to the Point Summary Charts. Write the points in the box for Lesson 31. ✔

Skipping Note: Check the students' errors from Lesson 31. If no more than 1 fourth of the students made more than 4 errors, skip this lesson and proceed with Lesson 33.

EXERCISE 1

Multiplication/Addition/Subtraction

a. Turn to Lesson 32.
- Look at the problems in Part 1.
- In some of these problems, you add or subtract. In some of the problems, you multiply.
b. When you add or subtract, you have to be able to rewrite the problem. When you multiply, you multiply top times the top and bottom times the bottom.
- First I want you to tell me whether the problem is the kind you can rewrite to add or subtract or the kind you multiply top times the top and bottom times the bottom.
c. Touch the first problem.
- Do you rewrite to add or subtract or do you multiply top times the top and bottom times the bottom? (Signal.) *Multiply top times the top and bottom times the bottom.*
d. Touch the next problem.
- Do you rewrite to add or subtract or do you multiply top times the top and bottom times the bottom? (Signal.) *Rewrite to add or subtract.*
e. Touch the next problem.
- Do you rewrite to add or subtract or do you multiply top times the top and bottom times the bottom? (Signal.) *Multiply top times the top and bottom times the bottom.*
f. Work all of the problems in Part 1. If the problem is the kind you can rewrite to add or subtract, work it the fast way. Remember to write the line in the answer. You have 10 minutes.
- (Observe students and give feedback.)

EXERCISE 2

Workcheck

a. We're going to check the answers. Exchange workbooks, and get ready to check the answers. (Pause.)
- Put an **X** next to each problem that the person misses.
- (Check and correct. See *Answer Key.*)
- Return the workbooks.
b. Now we're going to figure out the number of points you've earned for this lesson.
- (Point to the posted information.)

Worksheet Items	Errors	Points
	0–2	10
	3	7
	4	5
	5	3
	6	1
	7 or more	0

- Count the number of items you got wrong. Figure out the number of points you earned and write the number in the "Items" box.
- (Observe students and give feedback.)
c. (Tell the group how many points they earned for the lesson.) Write that number in the "Hard Work" box; then figure out the total for today's lesson.
d. Turn to the Point Summary Charts. Write the points in the box for Lesson 32. ✔

EXERCISE 1

Multiplication/Addition/Subtraction

a. Turn to Lesson 33.
- Look at the problems in Part 1.
- In some of these problems, you add or subtract. In some of the problems, you multiply.

b. When you add or subtract, you have to be able to rewrite the problem. When you multiply, you multiply top times the top and bottom times the bottom.
- First I want you to tell me whether the problem is the kind you can rewrite to add or subtract or the kind you multiply top times the top and bottom times the bottom.

c. Touch the first problem.
- Do you rewrite to add or subtract or do you multiply top times the top and bottom times the bottom? (Signal.) *Rewrite to add or subtract.*

d. Touch the next problem.
- Do you rewrite to add or subtract or do you multiply top times the top and bottom times the bottom? (Signal.) *Rewrite to add or subtract.*

e. Touch the next problem.
- Do you rewrite to add or subtract or do you multiply top times the top and bottom times the bottom? (Signal.) *Multiply top times the top and bottom times the bottom.*

f. Work all of the problems in Part 1. If the problem is the kind you can rewrite to add or subtract, work it the fast way. Remember to write the line in the answer. You have 7 minutes.
- (Observe students and give feedback.)

EXERCISE 2

Addition/Subtraction

a. (Write on the board:)
★

$$\frac{2}{3} + \frac{5}{3} \qquad \frac{8}{7} - \frac{3}{8} \qquad \frac{9}{6} - \frac{4}{6} \qquad \frac{6}{7} + \frac{3}{7}$$

b. When can you add or subtract fractions? (Signal.) *When the wholes are the same.*
- We're going to learn to add and subtract fractions when they are written like this.

c. I'll point and you read the problem.
- (Touch each part as the students read.) *2 thirds plus 5 thirds.*
- You can add those fractions the way they are because the wholes are the same.

d. What will I write on the bottom for the answer? (Signal.) *3.*
- (Write to show:)

$$\frac{2}{3} + \frac{5}{3} = \frac{}{3} \qquad \frac{8}{7} - \frac{3}{8} \qquad \frac{9}{6} - \frac{4}{6} \qquad \frac{6}{7} + \frac{3}{7}$$

- The top is 2 plus 5. What does that equal? (Signal.) *7.*
- I'll write that in for the top of the answer.
- (Write to show:)

$$\frac{2}{3} + \frac{5}{3} = \frac{7}{3} \qquad \frac{8}{7} - \frac{3}{8} \qquad \frac{9}{6} - \frac{4}{6} \qquad \frac{6}{7} + \frac{3}{7}$$

- Tell me the whole answer to the problem. (Signal.) *7 thirds.*

e. Read the next problem.
- (Touch each part as the students read.) *8 sevenths minus 3 eighths.*
- Can we subtract these fractions the way they are? (Signal.) *No.*
- Why not? (Signal.) *The wholes aren't the same.*

f. Read the next problem.
- (Touch each part as the students read.) *9 sixths minus 4 sixths.*
- Can we subtract these fractions the way they are? (Signal.) *Yes.*
- You can subtract those fractions the way they are because the wholes are the same.

g. What will I write on the bottom for the answer? (Signal.) *6.*
- (Write to show:)

$$+\frac{\frac{2}{3}}{\frac{5}{3}} \quad -\frac{\frac{8}{7}}{\frac{3}{8}} \quad -\frac{\frac{9}{6}}{\frac{4}{6}} \quad +\frac{\frac{6}{7}}{\frac{3}{7}}$$
$$\frac{7}{3} \qquad\qquad\qquad \overline{6}$$

- The top is 9 minus 4. What does that equal? (Signal.) *5.*
- I'll write that in for the top of the answer.
- (Write to show:)

$$+\frac{\frac{2}{3}}{\frac{5}{3}} \quad -\frac{\frac{8}{7}}{\frac{3}{8}} \quad -\frac{\frac{9}{6}}{\frac{4}{6}} \quad +\frac{\frac{6}{7}}{\frac{3}{7}}$$
$$\frac{7}{3} \qquad\qquad\qquad \frac{5}{6}$$

- Tell me the whole answer to the problem. (Signal.) *5 sixths.*

h. Read the last problem.
- (Touch each part as the students read.) *6 sevenths plus 3 sevenths.*
- Can we add these fractions the way they are? (Signal.) *Yes.*
- You can add those fractions the way they are because the wholes are the same.

i. What will I write on the bottom for the answer? (Signal.) *7.*
- (Write to show:)

$$+\frac{\frac{2}{3}}{\frac{5}{3}} \quad -\frac{\frac{8}{7}}{\frac{3}{8}} \quad -\frac{\frac{9}{6}}{\frac{4}{6}} \quad +\frac{\frac{6}{7}}{\frac{3}{7}}$$
$$\frac{7}{3} \qquad\qquad\qquad \frac{5}{6} \qquad \overline{7}$$

- The top is 6 plus 3. What does that equal? (Signal.) *9.*
- I'll write that in for the top of the answer.
- (Write to show:)

$$+\frac{\frac{2}{3}}{\frac{5}{3}} \quad -\frac{\frac{8}{7}}{\frac{3}{8}} \quad -\frac{\frac{9}{6}}{\frac{4}{6}} \quad +\frac{\frac{6}{7}}{\frac{3}{7}}$$
$$\frac{7}{3} \qquad\qquad\qquad \frac{5}{6} \qquad \frac{9}{7}$$

- Tell me the whole answer to the problem. (Signal.) *9 sevenths.*

j. Look at the problems in Part 2. Figure out the answers to all of the problems you can work. Skip the problems you can't work. You have 3 minutes.
- (Observe students and give feedback.)

EXERCISE 3

Workcheck

a. We're going to check the answers. Exchange workbooks, and get ready to check the answers. (Pause.)
- Put an **X** next to each problem that the person misses.
- (Check and correct. See **Answer Key.**)
- Return the workbooks.

b. Now we're going to figure out the number of points you've earned for this lesson.
- (Point to the posted information.)

Worksheet Items	Errors	Points
	0–2	10
	3	7
	4	5
	5	3
	6	1
	7 or more	0

- Count the number of items you got wrong. Figure out the number of points you earned and write the number in the "Items" box.
- (Observe students and give feedback.)

c. (Tell the group how many points they earned for the lesson.) Write that number in the "Hard Work" box; then figure out the total for today's lesson.

d. Turn to the Point Summary Charts. Write the points in the box for Lesson 33. ✔

EXERCISE 1

Multiplication/Addition/Subtraction

a. Turn to Lesson 34.
- Look at the problems in Part 1.
- In some of these problems, you add or subtract. In some of these problems, you multiply.

b. When you multiply, you multiply top times the top and bottom times the bottom. When you add or subtract, you may work the problems the fast way without rewriting them. Be sure to look at the sign for the problem. You won't be able to do some of the problems that tell you to add or subtract.

c. Work all of the problems in Part 1. You have 4 minutes.
- (Observe students and give feedback.)

EXERCISE 2

Addition/Subtraction

a. (Write on the board:)
★

$$-\frac{9}{5}\ \frac{3}{5} \qquad +\frac{8}{3}\ \frac{3}{8} \qquad +\frac{6}{4}\ \frac{9}{4}$$

b. When can you add or subtract fractions? (Signal.) *When the wholes are the same.*
- We're going to work some problems when they are written like this.

c. I'll point and you read the problem.
- (Touch each part as the students read.) *9 fifths minus 3 fifths.*
- You can subtract those fractions the way they are because the wholes are the same.

d. What will I write on the bottom for the answer? (Signal.) *5.*

- (Write to show:)

$$-\frac{9}{5}\ \frac{3}{5}\ \overline{5} \qquad +\frac{8}{3}\ \frac{3}{8} \qquad +\frac{6}{4}\ \frac{9}{4}$$

- The top says 9 minus 3. What does that equal? (Signal.) *6.*
- I'll write that in for the top of the answer.
- (Write to show:)

$$-\frac{9}{5}\ \frac{3}{5}\ \frac{6}{5} \qquad +\frac{8}{3}\ \frac{3}{8} \qquad +\frac{6}{4}\ \frac{9}{4}$$

- Tell me the whole answer to the problem. (Signal.) *6 fifths.*

e. Read the next problem.
- (Touch each part as the students read.) *8 thirds plus 3 eighths.*
- Can we add these fractions the way they are? (Signal.) *No.*
- Why not? (Signal.) *The wholes aren't the same.*

f. Read the last problem.
- (Touch each part as the students read.) *6 fourths plus 9 fourths.*
- You can add those fractions the way they are because the wholes are the same.

g. What will I write on the bottom for the answer? (Signal.) *4.*
- (Write to show:)

$$-\frac{9}{5}\ \frac{3}{5}\ \frac{6}{5} \qquad +\frac{8}{3}\ \frac{3}{8} \qquad +\frac{6}{4}\ \frac{9}{4}\ \overline{4}$$

- The top says 6 plus 9. What does that equal? (Signal.) *15.*
- I'll write that in for the top of the answer.
- (Write to show:)

$$\begin{array}{ccc}
\dfrac{9}{5} & \dfrac{8}{3} & \dfrac{6}{4} \\[6pt]
-\dfrac{3}{5} & +\dfrac{3}{8} & +\dfrac{9}{4} \\[6pt]
\hline
\dfrac{6}{5} & & \dfrac{\boxed{15}}{4}
\end{array}$$

- Tell me the whole answer to the problem. (Signal.) *15 fourths*

h. Look at the problems in Part 2. Figure out the answers to all of the problems you can work. Skip the problems you can't work. You have 2 minutes.
- (Observe students and give feedback.)

EXERCISE 3

Multiplication

a. Touch the first problem in Part 3.
- This problem is written a new way. Read the problem. (Signal.) *2 thirds times 4 fifths.*

b. How do you multiply fractions? (Signal.) *The top times the top and bottom times the bottom.*

c. Do you have to write any numbers as fractions before you multiply? (Signal.) *No.*

d. Read top times the top. (Signal.) *2 times 4.*
- What does top times the top equal? (Signal.) *8.*
- Below the line at the bottom of the problem, write that for the top part of the answer.
- Write the fraction line for the answer.

e. Read bottom times the bottom. (Signal.) *3 times 5.*
- What does bottom times the bottom equal? (Signal.) *15.*
- Write that for the bottom part of the answer. ✔

f. Read the next problem. (Signal.) *3 fifths times 4.*

g. (write on the board:)

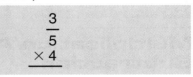

$$\begin{array}{c}
\dfrac{3}{5} \\[4pt]
\times\ 4 \\
\hline
\end{array}$$

h. (Write to show:)

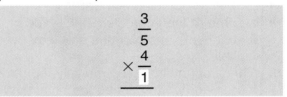

$$\begin{array}{c}
\dfrac{3}{5} \\[4pt]
\times\ \dfrac{4}{1} \\
\hline
\end{array}$$

- Here's what you should have.
- Do you have to write any numbers as fractions before you multiply? (Signal.) *Yes.*
- What number do you have to write as a fraction? (Signal.) *4.*
- Do it. ✔

i. Read top times the top. (Signal.) *3 times 4.*
- What does top times the top equal? (Signal.) *12.*
- Below the line at the bottom of the problem, write that for the top part of the answer.
- Write the fraction line for the answer.

j. Read bottom times the bottom. (Signal.) *5 times 1.*
- What does bottom times the bottom equal? (Signal.) *5.*
- Write that for the bottom part of the answer.

k. Read the next problem. (Signal.) *5 times 2 sevenths.*

l. Do you have to write any numbers as fractions before you multiply? (Signal.) *Yes.*
- Do it. ✔
- What does top times the top equal? (Signal.) *10.*
- Write it below for the answer. ✔
- Write the fraction line in the answer.

m. What does bottom times the bottom equal? (Signal.) *7.*
- Write it in the answer.
- What's the answer to the problem? (Signal.) *10 sevenths.*

n. Work the rest of the problems in Part 3. You have 4 minutes.
- (Observe students and give feedback.)

EXERCISE 4

Workcheck

a. We're going to check the answers. Exchange workbooks, and get ready to check the answers. (Pause.)
- Put an **X** next to each problem that the person misses.
- (Check and correct. See *Answer Key*.)
- Return the workbooks.

b. Now we're going to figure out the number of points you've earned for this lesson.
- (Point to the posted information.)

Worksheet Items	Errors	Points
	0–2	10
	3	7
	4	5
	5	3
	6	1
	7 or more	0

- Count the number of items you got wrong. Figure out the number of points you earned and write the number in the "Items" box.
- (Observe students and give feedback.)

c. (Tell the group how many points they earned for the lesson.) Write that number in the "Hard Work" box; then figure out the total for today's lesson.

d. Turn to the Point Summary Charts. Write the points in the box for Lesson 34. ✔

EXERCISE 1

Multiplication/Addition/Subtraction

a. Turn to Lesson 35.
- Look at the problems Part 1.
- In some of these problems, you add or subtract. In some of the problems, you multiply.

b. When you multiply, you multiply top times the top and bottom times the bottom. When you add or subtract, you may work the problems the fast way without rewriting them. You won't be able to do some of the problems that tell you to add or subtract.

c. Work all of the problems in Part 1. You have 1 minute.
- (Observe students and give feedback.)

EXERCISE 2

Addition/Subtraction

a. (Write on the board:)
★
$$+\frac{5}{7} \quad +\frac{3}{7} \qquad +\frac{3}{8} \quad +\frac{2}{7}$$

b. When can you add or subtract fractions? (Signal.) *When the wholes are the same.*
- We're going to work some problems when they are written like this.

c. I'll point and you read the problem.
- (Touch each part as the students read.) *5 sevenths plus 3 sevenths.*
- Can we add those fractions the way they are? (Signal.) *Yes.*

d. What will I write on the bottom for the answer? (Signal.) *7.*

- (Write to show:)
$$\frac{\frac{5}{7}}{+\frac{3}{7}} \qquad \frac{\frac{3}{8}}{+\frac{2}{7}}$$
$$\frac{}{7}$$

- The top is 5 plus 3. What does that equal? (Signal.) *8.*
- I'll write that in for the top of the answer.
- (Write to show:)
$$\frac{\frac{5}{7}}{+\frac{3}{7}} \qquad \frac{\frac{3}{8}}{+\frac{2}{7}}$$
$$\frac{8}{7}$$

- Tell me the whole answer to the problem. (Signal.) *8 sevenths.*

e. Read the next problem.
- (Touch each part as the students read.) *3 eighths plus 2 sevenths.*
- Can we add these fractions the way they are? (Signal.) *No.*
- Why not? (Signal.) *The wholes aren't the same.*

f. Look at the problems in Part 2. Figure out the answers to all of the problems you can work. Skip the problems you can't work. You have 4 minutes.
- (Observe students and give feedback.)

EXERCISE 3

Multiplication

a. Touch the first problem in Part 3.
- This problem is written a new way. Read the problem. (Signal.) *2 fifths times 4 sevenths.*

b. How do you multiply fractions? (Signal.) *The top times the top and bottom times the bottom.*

c. Do you have to write any numbers as fractions before you multiply? (Signal.) *No.*

d. Read top times the top. (Signal.) *2 times 4.*
- What does top times the top equal? (Signal.) *8.*
- Below the line at the bottom of the problem, write that for the top part of the answer. ✔
- Write the fraction line in the answer. ✔

e. Read bottom times the bottom. (Signal.) *5 times 7.*
- What does bottom times the bottom equal? (Signal.) *35.*
- Write that for the bottom part of the answer.

f. Read the next problem. (Signal.) *4 thirds times 7.*

g. Do you have to write any numbers as fractions before you multiply? (Signal.) *Yes.*
- What number do you have to write as a fraction? (Signal.) *7.*
- Do it. ✔

h. Read top times the top. (Signal.) *4 times 7.*
- What does top times the top equal? (Signal.) *28.*
- Below the line at the bottom of the problem, write that for the top part of the answer.
- Write the fraction line for the answer.

i. Read bottom times the bottom. (Signal.) *3 times 1.*
- What does bottom times the bottom equal? (Signal.) *3.*
- Write that for the bottom part of the answer.

j. Work the rest of the problems in Part 3. You have 4 minutes.
- (Observe students and give feedback.)

EXERCISE 4

Workcheck

a. We're going to check the answers. Exchange workbooks, and get ready to check the answers. (Pause.)
- Put an **X** next to each problem that the person misses.
- (Check and correct. See *Answer Key.*)
- Return the workbooks.

b. Now we're going to figure out the number of points you've earned for this lesson.
- (Point to the posted information.)

Worksheet Items	Errors	Points
	0–2	10
	3	7
	4	5
	5	3
	6	1
	7 or more	0

- Count the number of items you got wrong. Figure out the number of points you earned and write the number in the "Items" box.
- (Observe students and give feedback.)

c. (Tell the group how many points they earned for the lesson.) Write that number in the "Hard Work" box; then figure out the total for today's lesson.

d. Turn to the Point Summary Charts. Write the points in the box for Lesson 35. ✔

e. Total your points for Lessons 31 through 35 and write the total number on the chart.
- (Observe students and give feedback.)

f. Everybody, find the Five-Lesson Point Graph. ✔
- (Help the students plot their five-lesson scores on the graph.)

EXERCISE 1

Multiplication/Addition/Subtraction

a. Turn to Lesson 36.
- Touch the first problem.
- What does the sign tell you to do? (Signal.) *Add.*

b. Can you add those fractions the way they are? (Signal.) *Yes.*
- Do it. ✔
- What's the answer? (Signal.) *11 fourths.*

c. Touch the next problem.
- What does the sign tell you to do? (Signal.) *Multiply.*
- Do you have to change any numbers to fractions before you multiply? (Signal.) *Yes.*
- Do it. ✔
- Now read top times the top. (Signal.) *5 times 6.*
- Read bottom times the bottom. (Signal.) *3 times 1.*
- Work the problem. ✔
- What's the answer? (Signal.) *30 thirds.*

d. Touch the next problem.
- What does the sign tell you to do? (Signal.) *Subtract.*
- Can you subtract those fractions the way they are? (Signal.) *No.*
- Why not? (Signal.) *The wholes aren't the same.*
- So you skip that problem.

e. Work the rest of the problems in Part 1. You can't work some of the problems that tell you to add or subtract. You have 10 minutes.
- (Observe students and give feedback.)

EXERCISE 2

Workcheck

a. We're going to check the answers. Exchange workbooks, and get ready to check the answers. (Pause.)
- Put an **X** next to each problem that the person misses.
- (Check and correct. See **Answer Key.)**
- Return the workbooks.

b. Now we're going to figure out the number of points you've earned for this lesson.
- (Point to the posted information.)

Worksheet Items	Errors	Points
	0–2	10
	3	7
	4	5
	5	3
	6	1
	7 or more	0

- Count the number of items you got wrong. Figure out the number of points you earned and write the number in the "Items" box.
- (Observe students and give feedback.)

c. (Tell the group how many points they earned for the lesson.) Write that number in the "Hard Work" box; then figure out the total for today's lesson.

d. Turn to the Point Summary Charts. Write the points in the box for Lesson 36. ✔

Lesson 37

EXERCISE 1

Multiplying by 1

a. Here's a rule. When you multiply by 1, you start and end with equal amounts. Listen again. When you multiply by 1, you start and end with equal amounts.

b. (Write on the board:)

$$4 \times 1 =$$

c. Are you multiplying by 1 in this problem? (Signal.) *Yes.*
- What other number do you start with? (Signal.) *4.*
- You're multiplying by 1, so you know the amount that you'll end with is equal to 4.
- Tell me the amount you'll end with. (Signal.) *4.*

d. (Write on the board:)

$$1 \times 7 =$$

e. Are you multiplying by 1 in this problem? (Signal.) *Yes.*
- What other number do you start with? (Signal.) *7.*
- You're multiplying by 1. Tell me the amount you'll end with. (Signal.) *7.*
- Yes, you'll end with an amount that is equal to 7.

f. (Write on the board:)

$$\frac{4}{5} \times 1 =$$

g. Are you multiplying by 1 in this problem? (Signal.) *Yes.*
- What other number do you start with? (Signal.) *4 fifths.*
- Tell me the amount you'll end with. (Signal.) *4 fifths.*
- Yes, you'll end with an amount that is equal to 4 fifths because you're multiplying by 1.

h. (Touch $4 \times 1 =$.)
- In this problem, you're multiplying by 1. You start with 4. Tell me the amount you end with. (Signal.) *4.*
- Yes, it equals 4.

- (Write to show:)

$$4 \times 1 = \boxed{4}$$

i. You know it equals the same amount you start with **because** you're multiplying by 1.
- How do you know you'll end with the same amount you start with? (Signal.) *You're multiplying by 1.*
- (Repeat until firm.)

j. (Touch $1 \times 7 =$.)
- In this problem, you are multiplying by 1. You start with 7. Tell me the amount you end with. (Signal.) *7.*
- How do you know you'll end with the same amount you start with? (Signal.) *You're multiplying by 1.*

k. (Touch $\frac{4}{5} \times 1 =$.)
- In this problem, you are multiplying by 1. You start with 4 fifths. Tell me the amount you end with. (Signal.) *4 fifths.*
- How do you know you'll end with the same amount you start with? (Signal.) *You're multiplying by 1.*

EXERCISE 2

Multiplication/Addition/Subtraction

a. Turn to Lesson 37. Touch the first problem.
- What does the sign tell you to do? (Signal.) *Add.*

b. Can you add those fractions the way they are? (Signal.) *Yes.*
- Do it.
- What's the answer? (Signal.) *8 sixths.*

c. Touch the next problem.
- What does the sign tell you to do? (Signal.) *Multiply.*
- Do you have to change any numbers to fractions before you multiply? (Signal.) *Yes.*
- Do it.
- Now multiply the top and bottom numbers. Work the problem.
- What's the answer? (Signal.) *10 thirds.*

d. Touch the next problem.

- What does the sign tell you to do? (Signal.) *Subtract.*
- Can you subtract those fractions the way they are? (Signal.) *Yes.*
- Do it.
- What's the answer? (Signal.) *6 thirds.*

e. Work the rest of the problems in Part 1. Remember, if you can't work a problem, skip it. You have 10 minutes.
- (Observe students and give feedback.)

EXERCISE 3

Workcheck

a. We're going to check the answers. Exchange workbooks, and get ready to check the answers. (Pause.)
- Put an **X** next to each problem that the person misses.
- (Check and correct. See **Answer Key.**)
- Return the workbooks.

b. Now we're going to figure out the number of points you've earned for this lesson.
- (Point to the posted information.)

Worksheet Items	Errors	Points
	0–2	10
	3	7
	4	5
	5	3
	6	1
	7 or more	0

- Count the number of items you got wrong. Figure out the number of points you earned and write the number in the "Items" box.
- (Observe students and give feedback.)

c. (Tell the group how many points they earned for the lesson.) Write that number in the "Hard Work" box; then figure out the total for today's lesson.

d. Turn to the Point Summary Charts. Write the points in the box for Lesson 37. ✔

Lesson 38

Skipping Note: Check the students' errors from Lesson 37. If no more than 1 fourth of the students made more than 4 errors, skip this lesson and proceed with Lesson 39.

EXERCISE 1
Multiplying by 1

a. (Write on the board:)

★

$$1 \times 8 =$$

b. Remember the rule. When you are multiplying by 1, you start and end with equal amounts.

c. Are you multiplying by 1 in this problem? (Signal.) *Yes.*
- What other number do you start with? (Signal.) *8.*
- Tell me the amount you'll end with. (Signal.) *8.*
- (Write to show:)

$$1 \times 8 = 8$$

- How do you know you'll end with the same amount you start with? (Signal.) *You're multiplying by 1.*

d. (Write on the board:)

$$6 \times 1 =$$

- Are you multiplying by 1 in this problem? (Signal.) *Yes.*
- What other number do you start with? (Signal.) *6.*
- Tell me the amount you'll end with. (Signal.) *6.*
- (Write to show:)

$$6 \times 1 = 6$$

- How do you know you'll end with the same amount you start with? (Signal.) *You're multiplying by 1.*

e. (Write on the board:)

$$\frac{2}{3} \times 1 =$$

- Are you multiplying by 1 in this problem? (Signal.) *Yes.*
- What other number do you start with? (Signal.) *2 thirds.*
- Tell me the amount you'll end with. (Signal.) *2 thirds.*
- (Write to show:)

$$\frac{2}{3} \times 1 = \frac{2}{3}$$

- How do you know you'll end with the same amount you start with? (Signal.) *You're multiplying by 1.*

f. (Write on the board:)

$$1 \times \frac{5}{2} =$$

- Are you multiplying by 1 in this problem? (Signal.) *Yes.*
- What other number do you start with? (Signal.) *5 halves.*
- Tell me the amount you'll end with. (Signal.) *5 halves.*
- (Write to show:)

$$1 \times \frac{5}{2} = \frac{5}{2}$$

- How do you know you'll end with the same amount you start with? (Signal.) *You're multiplying by 1.*

EXERCISE 2

Multiplication/Addition/Subtraction

a. Turn to Lesson 38.
- Touch the first problem in Part 1.
- What does the sign tell you to do? (Signal.) *Add.*

b. Can you add those fractions the way they are? (Signal.) *Yes.*
- Do it. ✔
- What's the answer? (Signal.) *9 fourths.*

c. Touch the next problem.
- What does the sign tell you to do? (Signal.) *Multiply.*
- Do you have to change any numbers to fractions in this problem? (Signal.) *Yes.*
- Do it. ✔
- Now multiply the top and multiply the bottom numbers. Work the problem. ✔
- What's the answer? (Signal.) *35 fourths.*

d. Touch the next problem.
- What does the sign tell you to do? (Signal.) *Subtract.*
- Can you subtract those fractions the way they are? (Signal.) *Yes.*
- Do it. ✔
- What's the answer? (Signal.) *3 fifths.*

e. Work the rest of the problems in Part 1. Remember, if you can't work a problem, skip it. You have 8 minutes.
- (Observe students and give feedback.)

EXERCISE 3

Numbers as Fractions

a. Touch the first problem in Part 2.
- The first fraction is 6 over 6. How many wholes does that equal? (Signal.) *1.*

b. Touch the next problem.
- The next fraction is 6 over 1. How many wholes does that equal? (Signal.) *6.*

c. In the next problem, there is a number. How do you write that number as a fraction? (Signal.) *6 over 1.*

d. Work all of the problems in Part 2. Write numbers for the fractions and write fractions for the numbers. You have 2 minutes.
- (Observe students and give feedback.)

EXERCISE 4

Workcheck

a. We're going to check the answers. Exchange workbooks, and get ready to check the answers. (Pause.)
- Put an **X** next to each problem that the person misses.
- (Check and correct. See **Answer Key.)**
- Return the workbooks.

b. Now we're going to figure out the number of points you've earned for this lesson.
- (Point to the posted information.)

Worksheet Items	Errors	Points
	0–2	10
	3	7
	4	5
	5	3
	6	1
	7 or more	0

- Count the number of items you got wrong. Figure out the number of points you earned and write the number in the "Items" box.
- (Observe students and give feedback.)

c. (Tell the group how many points they earned for the lesson.) Write that number in the "Hard Work" box; then figure out the total for today's lesson.

d. Turn to the Point Summary Charts. Write the points in the box for Lesson 38. ✔

EXERCISE 1

Multiplying by 1

a. (Write on the board:)

★

$$\frac{4}{3} \times 1 =$$

b. Remember the rule. When you are multiplying by 1, you start and end with equal amounts.

c. (Touch the first problem.)
- Are you multiplying by 1 in this problem? (Signal.) *Yes.*
- What other number do you start with? (Signal.) *4 thirds.*
- Tell me the amount you'll end with. (Signal.) *4 thirds.*
- (Write to show:)

$$\frac{4}{3} \times 1 = \boxed{\frac{4}{3}}$$

- How do you know you'll end with the same amount you start with? (Signal.) *You're multiplying by 1.*

d. (Write on the board:)

$$1 \times 5 =$$

- Are you multiplying by 1 in this problem? (Signal.) *Yes.*
- What other number do you start with? (Signal.) *5.*
- Tell me the amount you'll end with. (Signal.) *5.*
- (Write to show:)

$$1 \times 5 = \boxed{5}$$

- How do you know you'll end with the same amount you start with? (Signal.) *You're multiplying by 1.*

e. (Write on the board:)

$$1 \times \frac{3}{4} =$$

- Are you multiplying by 1 in this problem? (Signal.) *Yes.*

- What other number do you start with? (Signal.) *3 fourths.*
- Tell me the amount you'll end with. (Signal.) *3 fourths.*
- (Write to show:)

$$1 \times \frac{3}{4} = \boxed{\frac{3}{4}}$$

- How do you know you'll end with the same amount you start with? (Signal.) *You're multiplying by 1.*

EXERCISE 2

Multiplying by 1

a. When a fraction equals 1, the top number is the same as the bottom number. You use the same number of parts that are in each whole.

b. I'll name some fractions that are equal to 1: 8 eighths. 5 fifths. 9 ninths. 3 thirds.

c. Your turn. Name some fractions that are equal to 1. (Call on individual students.)

d. I'll say more fractions. Some fractions will be equal to 1, and some will not be equal to 1. Don't be fooled.
- 5 fourths. Is that a fraction equal to 1? (Signal.) *No.*
- 7 sevenths. Is that a fraction equal to 1? (Signal.) *Yes.*
- 2 halves. Is that a fraction equal to 1? (Signal.) *Yes.*
- 10 sevenths. Is that a fraction equal to 1? (Signal.) *No.*
- 8 eighths. Is that a fraction equal to 1? (Signal.) *Yes.*

Lesson 39

EXERCISE 3

Numbers as Fractions

a. Turn to Lesson 39.
- Touch the first problem in Part 1.
- The first fraction is 12 over 1. How many wholes does that equal? (Signal.) *12.*

b. Touch the next problem.
- The next fraction is 5 over 5. How many wholes does that equal? (Signal.) *1.*

c. In the next problem, there is a number. How do you write that number as a fraction? (Signal.) *7 over 1.*

d. Work all of the problems in Part 1. Write numbers for the fractions and write fractions for the numbers. You have 2 minutes.
- (Observe students and give feedback.)

EXERCISE 4

Multiplication/Addition/Subtraction

a. Touch the first problem in Part 2.
- What does the sign tell you to do? (Signal.) *Add.*

b. Can you add those fractions the way they are? (Signal.) *Yes.*
- What do you do first? (Signal.) *Write the bottom number.*
- Then what do you do? (Signal.) *Add the top numbers.*
- Work the problem. ✔
- What's the answer? (Signal.) *12 fifths.*

c. Touch the next problem.
- What does the sign tell you to do? (Signal.) *Multiply.*
- What do you do first? (Signal.) *Check to change numbers to fractions.*
- Yes, check to change numbers to fractions.
- Do you have to change numbers in this problem? (Signal.) *Yes.*
- Do it. ✔
- Now what do you do? (Signal.) *Multiply the top and multiply the bottom.*
- Work the problem. ✔
- What's the answer? (Signal.) *21 eighths.*

d. Touch the next problem.
- What does the sign tell you to do? (Signal.) *Subtract.*
- Can you subtract those fractions the way they are? (Signal.) *Yes.*
- What do you do first? (Signal.) *Write the bottom number.*
- Then what do you do? (Signal.) *Subtract the top numbers.*
- Work the problem. ✔
- What's the answer? (Signal.) *10 thirds.*

e. Work the rest of the problems in Part 2. Remember, if you can't work a problem, skip it. You have 8 minutes.
- (Observe students and give feedback.)

EXERCISE 4

Workcheck

a. We're going to check the answers. Exchange workbooks, and get ready to check the answers. (Pause.)
- Put an **X** next to each problem that the person misses.
- (Check and correct. See **Answer Key.**)
- Return the workbooks.

b. Now we're going to figure out the number of points you've earned for this lesson.
- (Point to the posted information.)

Worksheet Items	Errors	Points
	0–2	10
	3	7
	4	5
	5	3
	6	1
	7 or more	0

- Count the number of items you got wrong. Figure out the number of points you earned and write the number in the "Items" box.
- (Observe students and give feedback.)

c. (Tell the group how many points they earned for the lesson.) Write that number in the "Hard Work" box; then figure out the total for today's lesson.

d. Turn to the Point Summary Charts. Write the points in the box for Lesson 39. ✔

94 Lesson 39

EXERCISE 1
Multiplying by 1

a. When a fraction equals 1, the top number is the same as the bottom number. You use the same number of parts that are in each whole.

b. I'll name some fractions that are equal to 1: 6 sixths. 4 fourths. 10 tenths.

c. Your turn. Name some fractions that are equal to 1. **(Call on individual students.)**

d. I'll say more fractions. Some fractions will be equal to 1. Some will not be equal to 1. Don't get fooled.

- 5 fifths. Is that a fraction equal to 1? (Signal.) *Yes.*
- 7 eighths. Is that a fraction equal to 1? (Signal.) *No.*
- 9 ninths. Is that a fraction equal to 1? (Signal.) *Yes.*
- 3 thirds. Is that a fraction equal to 1? (Signal.) *Yes.*
- 4 thirds. Is that a fraction equal to 1? (Signal.) *No.*

EXERCISE 2
Multiplying by 1

a. What's the rule about multiplying by 1? (Signal.) *You start and end with equal amounts.*

b. Let's name some fractions equal to 1.

- **(Call on 3 students.)**

c. (Write on the board:)

$$\frac{4}{5} \times \left(\right) =$$

- You're going to multiply by 1 in this problem. First we will write a fraction equal to 1 in the parentheses. Let's use 3 thirds.

d. (Write to show:)

$$\frac{4}{5} \times \left(\frac{3}{3} \right) =$$

e. What other number do we start with? (Signal.) *4 fifths.*

- Tell me the amount you'll end with. (Signal.) *4 fifths.*
- How do you know you'll end with the same amount you start with? (Signal.) *You're multiplying by 1.*

f. Let's work it. There are no numbers to change to fractions. What do we do next? (Signal.) *Multiply the top and multiply the bottom.*

- What does top times the top equal? (Signal.) *12.*
- (Write to show:)

$$\frac{4}{5} \times \left(\frac{3}{3} \right) = \frac{12}{}$$

- What does bottom times the bottom equal? (Signal.) *15.*
- (Write to show:)

$$\frac{4}{5} \times \left(\frac{3}{3} \right) = \frac{12}{15}$$

g. We multiplied 4 fifths by a fraction equal to 1. We ended with 12/15ths. Tell me the amount 12/15ths equals. (Signal.) *4 fifths.*

- How do you know you end with the same amount you start with? (Signal.) *You're multiplying by 1.*

h. (Write on the board:)

$$\frac{6}{3} \times \left(\right) =$$

- You're going to multiply by 1 in this problem. First we will write a fraction equal to 1 in the parentheses. Let's use 5 fifths.

i. (Write to show:)

$$\frac{6}{3} \times \left(\frac{5}{5} \right) =$$

j. What other number do we start with? (Signal.) *6 thirds.*

- Tell me the amount you'll end with. (Signal.) *6 thirds.*
- How do you know you'll end with the same amount you start with? (Signal.) *You're multiplying by 1.*

k. Let's work it. There are no numbers to change to fractions. What do we do next? (Signal.) *Multiply the top and multiply the bottom.*
- What does top times the top equal? (Signal.) *30.*
- (Write to show:)

$$\frac{6}{3} \times \left(\frac{5}{5}\right) = \frac{30}{}$$

- What does bottom times the bottom equal? (Signal.) *15.*
- (Write to show:)

$$\frac{6}{3} \times \left(\frac{5}{5}\right) = \frac{30}{15}$$

l. We multiplied 6 thirds by a fraction equal to 1. We ended with 30 fifteenths. Tell me the amount 30 fifteenths equals. (Signal.) *6 thirds.*
- How do you know you end with the same amount you start with? (Signal.) *You're multiplying by 1.*

m. (Write on the board:)

$$5 \times \left(\right) =$$

n. You're going to multiply by 1 in this problem. First we'll write a fraction equal to 1 in the parentheses. Let's use 2 halves.
- (Write to show:)

$$5 \times \left(\frac{2}{2}\right) =$$

- What other number do we start with? (Signal.) *5.*
- Tell me the amount you'll end with. (Signal.) *5.*

- How do you know you'll end with the same amount you start with? (Signal.) *You're multiplying by 1.*

o. Let's work it. Are there any numbers to change to fractions? (Signal.) *Yes.*
- (Write on the board:)

$$\frac{5}{1} \times \left(\frac{2}{2}\right) =$$

- What do we do next? (Signal.) *Multiply the top and multiply the bottom.*
- What does top times the top equal? (Signal.) *10.*
- (Write to show:)

$$\frac{5}{1} \times \left(\frac{2}{2}\right) = \frac{10}{}$$

- What does bottom times the bottom equal? (Signal.) *2.*
- (Write to show:)

$$\frac{5}{1} \times \left(\frac{2}{2}\right) = \frac{10}{2}$$

p. We multiplied 5 by a fraction equal to 1. We ended with 10 halves. Tell me the amount 10 halves equals. (Signal.) *5.*
- How do you know you end with the same amount you start with? (Signal.) *You're multiplying by 1.*

EXERCISE 3

Multiplication/Addition/ Subtraction

a. Turn to Lesson 40. Touch the first problem.
- What does the sign tell you to do? (Signal.) *Add.*
b. Can you add those fractions the way they are? (Signal.) *Yes.*
- What do you do first? (Signal.) *Write the bottom number.*
- Then what do you do? (Signal.) *Add the top numbers.*
- Work the problem. ✔
- What's the answer? (Signal.) *17 eighths.*
c. Touch the next problem.
- What does the sign tell you to do? (Signal.) *Multiply.*
- What do you do first? (Signal.) *Check to change numbers to fractions.*
- Do you have to change numbers in this problem? (Signal.) *Yes.*
- Do it. ✔
- Now what do you do? (Signal.) *Multiply the top and multiply the bottom.*
- Work the problem. ✔
- What's the answer? (Signal.) *35 fifths.*
d. Touch the next problem.
- What does the sign tell you to do? (Signal.) *Add.*
- Can you add those fractions the way they are? (Signal.) *No.*
- Why not? (Signal.) *The wholes aren't the same.*
- So you skip that problem.
e. Work the rest of the problems in Part 1. You have 10 minutes.
- (Observe students and give feedback.)

EXERCISE 4

Workcheck

a. We're going to check the answers. Exchange workbooks, and get ready to check the answers. (Pause.)
- Put an **X** next to each problem that the person misses.
- (Check and correct. See **Answer Key.**)
- Return the workbooks.
b. Now we're going to figure out the number of points you've earned for this lesson.
- (Point to the posted information.)

Worksheet Items	Errors	Points
	0–2	10
	3	7
	4	5
	5	3
	6	1
	7 or more	0

- Count the number of items you got wrong. Figure out the number of points you earned and write the number in the "Items" box.
- (Observe students and give feedback.)
c. (Tell the group how many points they earned for the lesson.) Write that number in the "Hard Work" box; then figure out the total for today's lesson.
d. Turn to the Point Summary Charts. Write the points in the box for Lesson 40. ✔
e. Total your points for Lessons 36 through 40 and write the total number on the chart.
- (Observe students and give feedback.)
f. Everybody, find the Five-Lesson Point Graph. ✔
- (Help the students plot their five-lesson scores on the graph.)

Lesson 41

EXERCISE 1
Multiplying by 1

a. What's the rule about multiplying by 1? (Signal.) *You start and end with equal amounts.*

b. Let's name some fractions equal to 1.
- (Call on 3 students.)

c. (Write on the board:)

$$\frac{4}{7} \times \left(\phantom{\frac{6}{6}} \right) =$$

- You're going to multiply by 1 in this problem. First we will write a fraction equal to 1 in the parentheses. Let's use 6 sixths.

d. (Write to show:)

$$\frac{4}{7} \times \left(\frac{6}{6} \right) =$$

e. What other number do we start with? (Signal.) *4 sevenths.*
- Tell me the amount you'll end with. (Signal.) *4 sevenths.*
- How do you know you'll end with the same amount you start with? (Signal.) *You're multiplying by 1.*

f. Let's work it. There are no numbers to change to fractions. What do we do next? (Signal.) *Multiply the top and multiply the bottom.*
- What does top times the top equal? (Signal.) *24.*
- (Write to show:)

$$\frac{4}{7} \times \left(\frac{6}{6} \right) = \frac{24}{}$$

- What does bottom times the bottom equal? (Signal.) *42.*
- (Write to show:)

$$\frac{4}{7} \times \left(\frac{6}{6} \right) = \frac{24}{42}$$

g. We multiplied 4/7ths by a fraction equal to 1. We ended with 24/42nds. Tell me the amount 24/42nds equals. (Signal.) *4/7ths.*
- How do you know you end with the same amount you start with? (Signal.) *You're multiplying by 1.*

h. (Write on the board:)

$$5 \times \left(\phantom{\frac{4}{4}} \right) =$$

i. You're going to multiply by 1 in this problem. First we'll write a fraction equal to 1 in the parentheses. Let's use 4 fourths.
- (Write to show:)

$$5 \times \left(\frac{4}{4} \right) =$$

- What other number do we start with? (Signal.) *5.*
- Tell me the amount you'll end with. (Signal.) *5.*
- How do you know you'll end with the same amount you start with? (Signal.) *You're multiplying by 1.*

j. Let's work it. Are there any numbers to change to fractions? (Signal.) *Yes.*
- (Write to show:)

$$\frac{5}{1} \times \left(\frac{4}{4} \right) =$$

- What do we do next? (Signal.) *Multiply the top and multiply the bottom.*
- What does top times the top equal? (Signal.) *20.*
- (Write to show:)

$$\frac{5}{1} \times \left(\frac{4}{4} \right) = \frac{20}{}$$

- What does bottom times the bottom equal? (Signal.) *4.*

- (Write to show:)

$$\frac{5}{1} \times \left(\frac{4}{4}\right) = \frac{20}{4}$$

k. We multiplied 5 by a fraction equal to 1. We ended with 20 fourths. Tell me the amount that 20 fourths equals. (Signal.) *5.*
- How do you know you end with the same amount you start with? (Signal.) *You're multiplying by 1.*

EXERCISE 2
Multiplying by 1

a. Turn to Lesson 41.
- Look at the fractions at the top of Part 1.
- Now look at the problems in Part 1.
- You're going to multiply a fraction equal to 1 in these problems. First you have to write a fraction in the parentheses.
b. Touch the first fraction equal to 1 in the row of fractions at the top of the page.
- What fraction equal to 1 will you use? (Signal.) *4 fourths.*
- Cross out that fraction. Then write that fraction in the parentheses of the first problem. ✔
- Tell me the amount you'll end with. (Signal.) *2 fifths.*
- How do you know it will equal 2 fifths? (Signal.) *You're multiplying by 1.*
- Figure out the answer when you multiply. (Pause.)
- What's the answer? (Signal.) *8/20ths.*
- Tell me the amount 8/20ths equals. (Signal.) *2 fifths.*
- Write **equals 2 fifths** at the end. ✔
- How do you know that 8/20ths equals 2 fifths? (Signal.) *You're multiplying by 1.*
c. Do the next problem. Cross out the next fraction that equals 1 at the top, and write that fraction in the parentheses of the second problem. Then work the problem. (Pause.)

- What's the answer when you multiply it? (Signal.) *12 thirds.*
- Tell me the amount that 12 thirds equals. (Signal.) *4.*
- Write **equals 4** at the end. ✔
- How do you know that 12 thirds equals 4? (Signal.) *You're multiplying by 1.*
d. Work the rest of the problems in Part 1. Use a new fraction equal to 1 for each problem. Cross out a fraction at the top as you use it. You have 4 minutes.
- (Observe students and give feedback.)

EXERCISE 3
Multiplication/Addition/ Subtraction

a. Touch the first problem in Part 2.
- What does the sign tell you to do? (Signal.) *Add.*
b. Can you add those fractions the way they are? (Signal.) *No.*
- Why not? (Signal.) *The wholes aren't the same.*
c. Touch the next problem.
- What does the sign tell you to do? (Signal.) *Multiply.*
- What do you have to do first? (Signal.) *Check to change numbers to fractions.*
- Do you have to do that in this problem? (Signal.) *Yes.*
- Do it. ✔
- Now what do you do? (Signal.) *Multiply the top and multiply the bottom.*
- Work the problem. ✔
- What's the answer? (Signal.) *10 thirds.*
d. Touch the next problem.
- What does the sign tell you to do? (Signal.) *Subtract.*
- Can you subtract those fractions the way they are? (Signal.) *Yes.*
- What do you do first? (Signal.) *Write the bottom number.*
- Then what do you do? (Signal.) *Subtract the top.*
- Work the problem. ✔
- What's the answer? (Signal.) *3 eighths.*

e. Work the rest of the problems in Part 2. You have 6 minutes.

- (Observe students and give feedback.)

EXERCISE 4

Workcheck

a. We're going to check the answers. Exchange workbooks, and get ready to check the answers. (Pause.)

- Put an **X** next to each problem that the person misses.
- (Check and correct. See *Answer Key.*)
- Return the workbooks.

b. Now we're going to figure out the number of points you've earned for this lesson.

- (Point to the posted information.)

Worksheet Items	Errors	Points
	0–2	10
	3	7
	4	5
	5	3
	6	1
	7 or more	0

- Count the number of items you got wrong. Figure out the number of points you earned and write the number in the "Items" box.
- (Observe students and give feedback.)

c. (Tell the group how many points they earned for the lesson.) Write that number in the "Hard Work" box; then figure out the total for today's lesson.

d. Turn to the Point Summary Charts. Write the points in the box for Lesson 41. ✔

Lesson 42

EXERCISE 1

Multiplying by 1

a. What's the rule about multiplying by 1? (Signal.) *You start and end with equal amounts.*

b. Let's name some fractions equal to 1.
- (Call on 3 students.)

c. (Write on the board:)

$$\frac{3}{4} \times \left(\quad\right) =$$

- You're going to multiply by 1 in this problem. First we will write a fraction equal to 1 in the parentheses. Let's use 5 fifths.

d. (Write to show:)

$$\frac{3}{4} \times \left(\frac{5}{5}\right) =$$

e. What other number do we start with? (Signal.) *3 fourths.*
- Tell me the amount you'll end with. (Signal.) *3 fourths.*
- How do you know you'll end with the same amount you start with? (Signal.) *You're multiplying by 1.*

f. Let's work it. There are no numbers to change to fractions. What do we do next? (Signal.) *Multiply the top and multiply the bottom.*
- What does top times the top equal? (Signal.) *15.*
- (Write to show:)

$$\frac{3}{4} \times \left(\frac{5}{5}\right) = \frac{15}{\quad}$$

- What does bottom times the bottom equal? (Signal.) *20.*
- (Write to show:)

$$\frac{3}{4} \times \left(\frac{5}{5}\right) = \frac{15}{20}$$

g. We multiplied 3 fourths by a fraction equal to 1. We ended with 15/20ths. Tell me the amount 15/20ths equals. (Signal.) *3 fourths.*
- How do you know you end with the same amount you start with? (Signal.) *You're multiplying by 1.*

h. Turn to Lesson 42.
- Look at the problems in Part 1.
- You're going to multiply by 1 in these problems. First you're going to write a fraction that equals 1 in the parentheses.
- Touch the first fraction equal to 1 at the top of Part 1.
- What fraction equal to 1 will you use first? (Signal.) *2 halves.*
- Cross out that fraction, and then write that fraction in the parentheses of the first problem. ✔
- What other number do you start with? (Signal.) *1 fourth.*
- Tell me the amount you'll end with. (Signal.) *1 fourth.*
- How do you know it will equal 1 fourth? (Signal.) *You're multiplying by 1.*
- Figure out the answer when you multiply. (Pause.)
- What's the answer? (Signal.) *2 eighths.*
- Tell me what 2 eighths equals. (Signal.) *1 fourth.*
- Write **equals 1 fourth** at the end. ✔
- How do you know that it equals 1 fourth? (Signal.) *You're multiplying by 1.*

i. Work the next problem. Cross out the next fraction that equals 1 at the top and use that fraction in the parentheses. Then work the problem. ✔
- What's the answer when you multiply? (Signal.) *14 sevenths.*
- Tell me the amount that 14 sevenths equals. (Signal.) *2.*
- Write **equals 2** at the end. ✔
- How do you know that it equals 2? (Signal.) *You're multiplying by 1.*

j. Work the rest of the problems in Part 1. Use a new fraction equal to 1 for each problem. Cross out a fraction at the top as you use it. You have 4 minutes.
- (Observe students and give feedback.)

EXERCISE 2

Multiplication/Addition/ Subtraction

a. Touch the first problem in Part 2.
- What does the sign tell you to do? (Signal.) *Multiply.*
b. What do you have to do first? (Signal.) *Check to change numbers to fractions.*
- Do you have to do that in this problem? (Signal.) *No.*
- Now what do you do? (Signal.) *Multiply the top and multiply the bottom.*
- Work the problem. ✔
- What's the answer? (Signal.) *70/15ths.*
c. Touch the next problem.
- What does the sign tell you to do? (Signal.) *Subtract.*
- Can you subtract those fractions the way they are? (Signal.) *No.*
- Why not? (Signal.) *The wholes aren't the same.*
d. Touch the next problem.
- What does the sign tell you to do? (Signal.) *Add.*
- Can you add those fractions the way they are? (Signal.) *Yes.*
- What do you do first? (Signal.) *Write the bottom number.*
- Then what do you do? (Signal.) *Add the top.*
- Work the problem. ✔
- What's the answer? (Signal.) *11 fifths.*
e. Work the rest of the problems in Part 2. You have 6 minutes.
- (Observe students and give feedback.)

EXERCISE 3

Fractions to Wholes

a. (Write on the board:)
★

$\frac{12}{4}$	$\frac{15}{3}$	$\frac{20}{2}$
$\frac{30}{5}$	$\frac{20}{4}$	

b. These fractions are the same as numbers. We're going to figure out the amount that each fraction equals.
- Here's a rule about fractions: A fraction equals 2 wholes when the top is 2 times bigger than the bottom.
- A fraction equals 5 wholes when the top is fives times bigger than the bottom.
- A fraction equals 6 wholes when the top is 6 times bigger than the bottom.
c. When does a fraction equal 3 wholes? (Signal.) *When the top is 3 times bigger than the bottom.*
- When does a fraction equal 9 wholes? (Signal.) *When the top is 9 times bigger than the bottom.*
- When does a fraction equal 7 wholes? (Signal.) *When the top is 7 times bigger than the bottom.*
d. (Point to $\frac{12}{4}$.)
- Let's figure out the number that this fraction equals. What's the bottom number? (Signal.) *4.*
- Tell me how many times bigger than 4 is the top. Get ready. (Signal.) *3.*

▶ **To Correct**
- (If the student has been taught to multiply by "count-bys," say:) Figure out how many times you would count by 4 to reach 12. (Pause.) What's the answer? (Signal.) *3.* ◀

▶ **To Correct**
- (If the student knows any other forms of multiplication, say:) Tell me 4 times how many equals twelve. (Pause.) What's the answer? (Signal.) *3.* ◀

e. The top is 3 times bigger than the bottom. So how many wholes does the fraction equal? (Signal.) *3.*
- Yes, it equals 3 wholes.

- (Write to show:)

$$\frac{12}{4} = 3$$

f. (Point to $\frac{15}{3}$.)

- Let's figure out the number that this fraction equals. What's the bottom number? (Signal.) *3.*
- Tell me how many times bigger than 3 is the top. Get ready. (Signal.) *5.*
- The top is 5 times bigger than the bottom. So how many wholes does the fraction equal? (Signal.) *5.*
- Yes, it equals 5 wholes.
- (Write to show:)

$$\frac{15}{3} = 5$$

g. (Point to $\frac{20}{2}$.)

- Let's figure out the number for this fraction. What's the bottom number? (Signal.) *2.*
- Tell me how many times bigger than 2 is the top. Get ready. (Signal.) *10.*
- So how many wholes does the fraction equal? (Signal.) *10.*
- (Write to show:)

$$\frac{20}{2} = 10$$

h. (Point to $\frac{30}{5}$.)

- What's the bottom number for this fraction? (Signal.) *5.*
- Tell me how many times bigger than 5 is the top. Get ready. (Signal.) *6.*
- So how many wholes does the fraction equal? (Signal.) *6.*
- (Write to show:)

$$\frac{30}{5} = 6$$

i. (Point to $\frac{20}{4}$.)

- What's the bottom number for this fraction? (Signal.) *4.*
- Tell me how many times bigger than 4 is the top. Get ready. (Signal.) *5.*
- So how many wholes does the fraction equal? (Signal.) *5.*
- (Write to show:)

$$\frac{20}{4} = 5$$

EXERCISE 4

Workcheck

a. We're going to check the answers. Exchange workbooks, and get ready to check the answers. (Pause.)

- Put an **X** next to each problem that the person misses.
- (Check and correct. See **Answer Key.**)
- Return the workbooks.

b. Now we're going to figure out the number of points you've earned for this lesson.

- (Point to the posted information.)

Worksheet Items	Errors	Points
	0–2	10
	3	7
	4	5
	5	3
	6	1
	7 or more	0

- Count the number of items you got wrong. Figure out the number of points you earned and write the number in the "Items" box.
- (Observe students and give feedback.)

c. (Tell the group how many points they earned for the lesson.) Write that number in the "Hard Work" box; then figure out the total for today's lesson.

d. Turn to the Point Summary Charts. Write the points in the box for Lesson 42. ✔

Lesson 43

EXERCISE 1

Multiplying by 1

a. What's the rule about multiplying by 1? (Signal.) *You start and end with equal amounts.*

b. (Write on the board:)

$$\frac{3}{4} \times \left(\right) =$$

- You're going to multiply by 1 in this problem. First we will write a fraction equal to 1 in the parentheses. Let's use 3 thirds.
- (Write to show:)

$$\frac{3}{4} \times \left(\frac{3}{3} \right) =$$

c. What other number do we start with? (Signal.) *3 fourths.*

- Tell me the amount you'll end with. (Signal.) *3 fourths.*
- How do you know you'll end with the same amount you start with? (Signal.) *You're multiplying by 1.*

d. Let's work it. There are no numbers to change to fractions. What do we do next? (Signal.) *Multiply the top and multiply the bottom.*

- What does top times the top equal? (Signal.) *9.*
- (Write to show:)

$$\frac{3}{4} \times \left(\frac{3}{3} \right) = \frac{9}{}$$

- What does bottom times the bottom equal? (Signal.) *12.*
- (Write to show:)

$$\frac{3}{4} \times \left(\frac{3}{3} \right) = \frac{9}{12}$$

e. We multiplied 3 fourths by a fraction equal to 1. We ended with 9 twelfths. Tell me the amount 9 twelfths equals. (Signal.) *3 fourths.*

- How do you know you end with the same amount you start with? (Signal.) *You're multiplying by 1.*

f. Turn to Lesson 43.

- Look at the problems in Part 1.
- You're going to multiply by 1 in these problems. First you're going to write a fraction that equals 1 in the parentheses.
- Touch the first fraction equal to 1 at the top of Part 1.
- What fraction equal to 1 will you use first? (Signal.) *5 fifths.*
- Cross out that fraction, and then write that fraction in the parentheses of the first problem. ✔
- What other number do you start with? (Signal.) *3 sevenths.*
- Tell me the amount you'll end with. (Signal.) *3 sevenths.*
- How do you know it will equal 3 sevenths? (Signal.) *You're multiplying by 1.*
- Figure out the answer when you multiply. (Pause.)
- What's the answer? (Signal.) *15/35ths.*
- Tell me what 15/35ths equals. (Signal.) *3 sevenths.*
- Write **equals 3 sevenths** at the end. ✔
- How do you know that it equals 3 sevenths? (Signal.) *You're multiplying by 1.*

g. Work the next problem. Cross out the next fraction that equals 1 at the top and use that fraction in the parentheses.

- Work the problem. ✔
- What's the answer when you multiply? (Signal.) *18 sixths.*
- Tell me the amount that 18 sixths equals. (Signal.) *3.*
- Write **equals 3**. ✔
- How do you know that it equals 3? (Signal.) *You're multiplying by 1.*

h. Work the rest of the problems in Part 1. Use a new fraction equal to 1 for each problem. Cross out a fraction at the top as you use it. You have 3 minutes.

• (Observe students and give feedback.)

EXERCISE 2

Fractions to Wholes

a. (Write on the board:)
★

$$\frac{10}{5} \qquad \frac{8}{2} \qquad \frac{24}{6}$$

$$\frac{16}{4} \qquad \frac{15}{3}$$

b. These fractions are the same as numbers. We're going to figure out the amount that each fraction equals.

• Here's a rule about fractions. A fraction equals 4 wholes when the top is 4 times bigger than the bottom.

• A fraction equals 8 wholes when the top is 8 times bigger than the bottom.

• A fraction equals 10 wholes when the top is 10 times bigger than the bottom.

c. When does a fraction equal 2 wholes? (Signal.) *When the top is 2 times bigger than the bottom.*

• When does a fraction equal 5 wholes? (Signal.) *When the top is 5 times bigger than the bottom.*

• When does a fraction equal 7 wholes? (Signal.) *When the top is 7 times bigger than the bottom.*

d. (Point to $\frac{10}{5}$.)

• Let's figure out the number that this fraction equals. What's the bottom number? (Signal.) *5.*

• Tell me how many times bigger than 5 is the top. Get ready. (Signal.) *2.*

▶ **To Correct**

• (If the student has been taught to multiply by "count-bys", say:) Figure out how many times you would count by 5 to reach 10. (Pause.) What's the answer? (Signal.) *2.* ◀

▶ **To Correct**

• (If the student knows any other forms of multiplication, say:) Tell me 5 times how many equals 10. (Pause.) What's the answer? (Signal.) *2.* ◀

e. The top is 2 times bigger than the bottom. So how many wholes does the fraction equal? (Signal.) *2.*

• Yes, it equals 2 wholes.

• (Write to show:)

$$\frac{10}{5} = 2$$

f. (Point to $\frac{8}{2}$.)

• Let's figure out the number that this fraction equals. What's the bottom number? (Signal.) *2.*

• Tell me how many times bigger than 2 is the top. Get ready. (Signal.) *4.*

• The top is 4 times bigger than the bottom. So how many wholes does the fraction equal? (Signal.) *4.*

• (Write to show:)

$$\frac{8}{2} = 4$$

g. (Point to $\frac{24}{6}$.)

• What's the bottom number for this fraction? (Signal.) *6.*

• Tell me how many times bigger than 6 is the top. (Pause. Signal.) *4.*

• So how many wholes does the fraction equal? (Signal.) *4.*

• (Write to show:)

$$\frac{24}{6} = 4$$

h. (Point to $\frac{16}{4}$.)

- What's the bottom number for this fraction? (Signal.) *4.*
- Tell me how many times bigger than 4 is the top. (Pause. Signal.) *4.*
- So how many wholes does the fraction equal? (Signal.) *4.*
- (Write to show:)

$$\frac{16}{4} = 4$$

i. (Point to $\frac{15}{3}$.)

- What's the bottom number for this fraction? (Signal.) *3.*
- Tell me how many times bigger than 3 is the top. Get ready. (Signal.) *5.*
- So how many wholes does the fraction equal? (Signal.) *5.*
- (Write to show:)

$$\frac{15}{3} = 5$$

EXERCISE 3

Multiplication/Addition/Subtraction

a. Touch the first problem in Part 2.
- What does the sign tell you to do? (Signal.) *Add.*

b. Can you add those fractions the way they are? (Signal.) *Yes.*
- What do you do first? (Signal.) *Write the bottom number.*
- Then what do you do? (Signal.) *Add the top.*
- Work the problem. ✔
- What's the answer? (Signal.) *11 eighths.*

c. Touch the next problem.
- What does the sign tell you to do? (Signal.) *Multiply.*
- What do you have to do first? (Signal.) *Check to change numbers to fractions.*
- Do you have to do that in this problem? (Signal.) *Yes.*

- Do it. ✔
- Now what do you do? (Signal.) *Multiply the top and multiply the bottom.*
- Work the problem. ✔
- What's the answer? (Signal.) *18 thirds.*

d. Touch the next problem.
- What does the sign tell you to do? (Signal.) *Subtract.*
- Can you subtract those fractions the way they are? (Signal.) *No.*
- Why not? (Signal.) *The wholes aren't the same.*
- So you skip that problem.

e. Work the rest of the problems in Part 2. You have 7 minutes.
- (Observe students and give feedback.)

EXERCISE 4

Workcheck

a. We're going to check the answers. Exchange workbooks, and get ready to check the answers. (Pause.)
- Put an **X** next to each problem that the person misses.
- (Check and correct. See **Answer Key.**)
- Return the workbooks.

b. Now we're going to figure out the number of points you've earned for this lesson.
- (Point to the posted information.)

Worksheet Items	Errors	Points
	0–2	10
	3	7
	4	5
	5	3
	6	1
	7 or more	0

- Count the number of items you got wrong. Figure out the number of points you earned and write the number in the "Items" box.
- (Observe students and give feedback.)

c. (Tell the group how many points they earned for the lesson.) Write that number in the "Hard Work" box; then figure out the total for today's lesson.

d. Turn to the Point Summary Charts. Write the points in the box for Lesson 43. ✔

Skipping Note: Check the students' errors from Lesson 43. If no more than 1 fourth of the students made more than 4 errors, skip this lesson and proceed with Lesson 45.

EXERCISE 1

Multiplying by 1

a. Turn to Lesson 44.
- Touch the first problem in Part 1.
- You have to multiply by a fraction that equals 1 in these problems. Cross out the first fraction at the top of Part 1 that equals 1 and put it in the parentheses of the first problem. ✔
- When you multiply in that problem, what will the end amount equal? (Signal.) *2 thirds.*
- How do you know that it will equal 2 thirds? (Signal.) *You're multiplying by 1.*

b. Work all of the problems in Part 1. Use a new fraction equal to 1 for each problem. Cross out a fraction as you use it. You have 2 minutes.
- (Observe students and give feedback.)

EXERCISE 2

Fractions to Wholes

a. Look at the problems in Part 2. You have to figure out how many wholes each fraction equals.

b. Touch the first fraction.
- What's the bottom number? (Signal.) *4.*
- Tell me how many times bigger than 4 is the top. Get ready. (Signal.) *3.*
- So how many wholes does the fraction equal? (Signal.) *3.*
- Write **equals 3**. ✔

c. Touch the next fraction.
- What's the bottom number? (Signal.) *7.*
- Tell me how many times bigger than 7 is the top. Get ready. (Signal.) *2.*
- So how many wholes does the fraction equal? (Signal.) *2.*
- Write **equals 2**. ✔

d. Work the rest of the problems in Part 2 the same way. You have 2 minutes.
- (Observe students and give feedback.)

EXERCISE 3

Multiplying by 1

a. (Write on the board:)
★

$$4 \times \left(\frac{7}{7} \right) =$$

$$3 \times \left(\frac{8}{8} \right) =$$

$$\left(\frac{2}{2} \right) \times 6 =$$

b. What's the rule about multiplying by 1? (Signal.) *You start and end with equal amounts.*

c. Let's work some problems and see whether we end with an equal amount.
- (Touch $4 \times \left(\frac{7}{7} \right)$.)
- Tell me what the amount you end with will equal. (Signal.) *4.*
- How do you know it will equal 4? (Signal.) *You're multiplying by 1.*

d. Let's multiply and see whether the answer is equal to 4.
- First I make 4 a fraction.
- (Write to show:)

$$\frac{4}{1} \times \left(\frac{7}{7} \right) =$$

- What does top times the top equal? (Signal.) *28.*
- (Write to show:)

$$\frac{4}{1} \times \left(\frac{7}{7} \right) = \frac{28}{}$$

- What does bottom times the bottom equal? (Signal.) *7.*

- (Write to show:)

$$\frac{4}{1} \times \left(\frac{7}{7}\right) = \frac{28}{7}$$

- (Touch the answer.) If this fraction equals four, the top number must be 4 times bigger than the bottom.
- Tell me how many times bigger than 7 is 28. Get ready. (Signal.) *4.*
- How many wholes does the fraction equal? (Signal.) *4.*
- The amount we end with equals the amount we start with. I can write **equals 4.**
- (Write to show:)

$$\frac{4}{1} \times \left(\frac{7}{7}\right) = \frac{28}{7} = 4$$

e. (Touch $3 \times \left(\frac{8}{8}\right)$.)

- Tell me the amount you'll end with. (Signal.) *3.*
- How do you know it will equal 3? (Signal.) *You're multiplying by 1.*
f. Let's multiply and see whether the answer is equal to 3.
- First I make 3 a fraction.
- (Write to show:)

$$\frac{3}{1} \times \left(\frac{8}{8}\right) =$$

- What does top times the top equal? (Signal.) *24.*
- (Write to show:)

$$\frac{3}{1} \times \left(\frac{8}{8}\right) = \frac{24}{}$$

- What does bottom times the bottom equal? (Signal.) *8.*
- (Write to show:)

$$\frac{3}{1} \times \left(\frac{8}{8}\right) = \frac{24}{8}$$

- (Touch the answer.) If this fraction equals 3, the top number must be 3 times bigger than the bottom.
- Tell me how many times bigger than 8 is 24. Get ready (Signal.) *3.*
- How many wholes does the fraction equal? (Signal.) *3.*
- The amount we end with equals the amount we start with. I can write **equals 3.**
- (Write to show:)

$$\frac{3}{1} \times \left(\frac{8}{8}\right) = \frac{24}{8} = 3$$

- What's the rule about multiplying by 1? (Signal.) *You start and end with equal amounts.*
g. Let's work another problem and see whether we end with an equal amount.
- (Touch $\left(\frac{2}{2}\right) \times 6 =$.)

- Tell me the amount you'll end with. (Signal.) *6.*
- How do you know it will equal 6? (Signal.) *You're multiplying by 1.*
h. Let's multiply and see whether the answer is equal to 6.
- First I make 6 a fraction.
- (Write to show:)

$$\left(\frac{2}{2}\right) \times \frac{6}{1} =$$

- What does top times the top equal? (Signal.) *12.*
- (Write to show:)

$$\left(\frac{2}{2}\right) \times \frac{6}{1} = \frac{12}{}$$

- What does bottom times the bottom equal? (Signal.) *2.*
- (Write to show:)

$$\left(\frac{2}{2}\right) \times \frac{6}{1} = \frac{12}{2}$$

Lesson 44

- (Touch the answer.) If this fraction equals six, the top number must be 6 times bigger than the bottom.
- How many times bigger than 2 is twelve? (Pause. Signal.) *6.*
- The amount we end with equals the amount we started with. I can write **equals 6.**
- (Write to show:)

$$\left(\frac{2}{2}\right) \times \frac{6}{1} = \frac{12}{2} = 6$$

EXERCISE 4

Multiplication/Addition/ Subtraction

a. Touch the first problem in Part 3.
- The problems tell you to add or subtract or multiply. Skip the problems you can't do. In some problems, you'll have to change numbers to fractions before you multiply.
b. Work all of the problems in Part 3. You have 6 minutes.
- (Observe students and give feedback.)

EXERCISE 5

Workcheck

a. We're going to check the answers. Exchange workbooks, and get ready to check the answers. (Pause.)
- Put an **X** next to each problem that the person misses.
- (Check and correct. See **Answer Key.**)
- Return the workbooks.
b. Now we're going to figure out the number of points you've earned for this lesson.
- (Point to the posted information.)

Worksheet Items	Errors	Points
	0–2	10
	3	7
	4	5
	5	3
	6	1
	7 or more	0

- Count the number of items you got wrong. Figure out the number of points you earned and write the number in the "Items" box.
- (Observe students and give feedback.)
c. (Tell the group how many points they earned for the lesson.) Write that number in the "Hard Work" box; then figure out the total for today's lesson.
d. Turn to the Point Summary Charts. Write the points in the box for Lesson 44. ✔

EXERCISE 1

Multiplying by 1

a. Turn to Lesson 45.
- Touch the first problem in Part 1.
- You have to multiply by a fraction that equals 1 in these problems. Cross out the first fraction at the top of Part 1 that equals 1 and put it in the parentheses of the first problem. ✔
- When you multiply in that problem, what will the end amount equal? (Signal.) *2 eighths.*
- How do you know that it will equal 2 eighths? (Signal.) *You're multiplying by 1.*

b. Work all of the problems in Part 1. Use a different fraction equal to 1 for each problem. Cross out a fraction at the top as you use it. You have 2 minutes.
- (Observe students and give feedback.)

EXERCISE 1

Fractions to Wholes

a. Now look at the problems in Part 2.
- You have to figure out the wholes that each fraction equals.

b. Touch the first fraction.
- What's the bottom number? (Signal.) *5.*
- Tell me how many times bigger than 5 is the top. Get ready. (Signal.) *3.*
- How many wholes does the fraction equal? (Signal.) *3.*
- Write **equals 3.** ✔

c. Touch the next fraction.
- What's the bottom number? (Signal.) *3.*
- Tell me how many times bigger than 3 is the top. Get ready. (Signal.) *8.*
- How many wholes does the fraction equal? (Signal.) *8.*
- Write **equals 8.** ✔

d. Work the rest of the problems in Part 2 the same way. You have 2 minutes.
- (Observe students and give feedback.)

EXERCISE 3

Multiplying by 1

a. (Write on the board:)
★

$$7 \times \left(\frac{3}{3} \right) =$$

$$2 \times \left(\frac{5}{5} \right) =$$

b. What's the rule about multiplying by 1? (Signal.) *You start and end with equal amounts.*

c. Let's work some problems and see whether we end with an equal amount.
- (Touch $7 \times \left(\frac{3}{3} \right)$.)
- Tell me what the amount you end with will equal? (Signal.) *7.*
- How do you know it will equal 7? (Signal.) *You're multiplying by 1.*

d. Let's multiply and see whether the answer is equal to 7.
- First I make 7 a fraction.
- (Write to show:)

$$\frac{7}{1} \times \left(\frac{3}{3} \right) =$$

- What does top times the top equal? (Signal.) *21.*
- (Write to show:)

$$\frac{7}{1} \times \left(\frac{3}{3} \right) = \underline{21}$$

- What does bottom times the bottom equal? (Signal.) *3.*
- (Write to show:)

$$\frac{7}{1} \times \left(\frac{3}{3} \right) = \frac{21}{3}$$

- (Touch the answer.) If this fraction equals 7, the top number must be 7 times bigger than the bottom.
- Tell me how many times bigger than 3 is 21? Get ready. (Signal.) *7.*
- How many wholes does the fraction equal? (Signal.) *7.*
- The amount we end with equals the amount we started with. I can write **equals 7.**
- (Write to show:)

$$\frac{7}{1} \times \left(\frac{3}{3}\right) = \frac{21}{3} = 7$$

e. (Touch $2 \times \left(\dfrac{5}{5}\right)$.)

- Tell me the amount you'll end with. (Signal.) *2.*
- How do you know it will equal 2? (Signal.) *You're multiplying by 1.*

f. Let's multiply and see whether the answer is equal to 2.

- First I make 2 a fraction.
- (Write on the board:)

$$\frac{2}{1} \times \left(\frac{5}{5}\right) =$$

- What does top times the top equal? (Signal.) *10.*
- (Write to show:)

$$\frac{2}{1} \times \left(\frac{5}{5}\right) = \frac{10}{}$$

- What does bottom times the bottom equal? (Signal.) *5.*
- (Write to show:)

$$\frac{2}{1} \times \left(\frac{5}{5}\right) = \frac{10}{5}$$

- (Touch the answer.) If this fraction equals 2, the top number must be 2 times bigger than the bottom.

- Tell me how many times bigger than 5 is 10. Get ready. (Signal.) *2.*
- How many wholes does the fraction equal? (Signal.) *2.*
- The amount we end with equals the amount we started with. I can write **equals 2.**
- (Write to show:)

$$\frac{2}{1} \times \left(\frac{5}{5}\right) = \frac{10}{5} = 2$$

EXERCISE 4

Expanding Fractions

a. (Write on the board:)

$$2\frac{1}{3} =$$

b. We're going to change this mixed number into a fraction.

- (Point to the $\dfrac{}{3}$.)
- The bottom number of the fraction tells us that we will have 3 parts in each whole. So I write a 3.
- (Write to show:)

$$2\frac{1}{3} = \frac{}{3}$$

- (Touch the 2.)
- How many wholes do we have? (Signal.) *2.*
- A fraction equals 2 wholes when the top is 2 times bigger than the bottom. What's the bottom of the fraction we're writing? (Signal.) *3.*
- The top must be 2 times bigger than 3. Tell me that number for the top. Get ready. (Signal.) *6.*
- (Write to show:)

$$2\frac{1}{3} = \frac{6}{3}$$

- We used the 2 wholes.

- (Touch the $\frac{1}{}$.)

- How many parts are left? (Signal.) *1.*
- (Write to show:)

$$2\frac{1}{3} = \frac{6+1}{3}$$

- We have 6 plus one parts. How many parts do we have altogether? (Signal.) *7.*
- (Write to show:)

$$2\frac{1}{3} = \frac{6+1}{3} = \frac{7}{}$$

- How many parts are in each whole? (Signal.) *3.*
- (Write to show:)

$$2\frac{1}{3} = \frac{6+1}{3} = \frac{7}{3}$$

- What fraction does 2 and one third equal? (Signal.) *7 thirds.*

New Problem

a. (Write on the board:)

$$3\frac{2}{4} =$$

b. We're going to change this mixed number into a fraction.

- (Point to the $\frac{}{4}$.)
- The bottom number of the fraction tells us that we will have 4 parts in each whole. So I write a 4.
- (Write to show:)

$$3\frac{2}{4} = \frac{}{4}$$

- (Touch the 3.)
- How many wholes do we have? (Signal.) *3.*
- A fraction equals 3 wholes when the top is 3 times bigger than the bottom. What's the bottom of the fraction we're writing? (Signal.) *4.*

- The top must be 3 times bigger than 4. Tell me the number for the top. (Pause. Signal.) *12.*
- (Write to show:)

$$3\frac{2}{4} = \frac{12}{4}$$

- We used 3 wholes.

- (Touch the $\frac{2}{}$.)

- How many parts are left? (Signal.) *2.*
- (Write to show:)

$$3\frac{2}{4} = \frac{12+2}{4}$$

c. We have 12 plus 2 parts. How many parts do we have altogether? (Signal.) *14.*
- (Write to show:)

$$3\frac{2}{4} = \frac{12+2}{4} = \frac{14}{}$$

- How many parts are in each whole? (Signal.) *4.*
- (Write to show:)

$$3\frac{2}{4} = \frac{12+2}{4} = \frac{14}{4}$$

- What fraction does 3 and 2 fourths equal? (Signal.) *14 fourths.*

New Problem

a. (Write on the board:)

$$4\frac{1}{2} =$$

b. Let's change this mixed number into a fraction.
- The bottom number of the fraction tells how many parts are in each whole.
- How many parts are in each whole? (Signal.) *2.*
- (Write on the board:)

$$4\frac{1}{2} = \frac{}{2}$$

- How many wholes do we have? (Signal.) *4.*
- A fraction equals 4 wholes when the top is how many times bigger than the bottom? (Signal.) *4.*
- What's the bottom of the fraction we're writing? (Signal.) *2.*
- So the top must be 4 times bigger than 2. Tell me the number for the top. Get ready. (Signal.) *8.*
- (Write to show:)

$$4\frac{1}{2} = \frac{8}{2}$$

- We used the 4 wholes. How many parts are left? (Signal.) *1.*
- (Write to show:)

$$4\frac{1}{2} = \frac{8+1}{2}$$

c. How many parts do we have altogether? (Signal.) *9.*
- (Write to show:)

$$4\frac{1}{2} = \frac{8+1}{2} = \frac{9}{}$$

- How many parts are in each whole? (Signal.) *2.*
- (Write to show:)

$$4\frac{1}{2} = \frac{8+1}{2} = \frac{9}{2}$$

- What fraction does 4 and one half equal? (Signal.) *9 halves.*

New Problem
a. (Write on the board:)

$$3\frac{2}{5} =$$

b. Let's change this mixed number into a fraction.
- How many parts are in each whole? (Signal.) *5.*

- (Write on the board:)

$$3\frac{2}{5} = \frac{}{5}$$

- How many wholes do we have? (Signal.) *3.*
- A fraction equals 3 wholes when the top is how many times bigger than the bottom? (Signal.) *3.*
- What's the bottom of the fraction we're writing? (Signal.) *5.*
- So the top must be 3 times bigger than 5. Tell me the number for the top. Get ready. (Signal.) *15.*
- (Write to show:)

$$3\frac{2}{5} = \frac{15}{5}$$

- We used 3 wholes. How many parts are left? (Signal.) *2.*
- (Write to show:)

$$3\frac{2}{5} = \frac{15+2}{5}$$

c. How many parts do we have altogether? (Signal.) *17.*
- (Write to show:)

$$3\frac{2}{5} = \frac{15+2}{5} = \frac{17}{}$$

- How many parts are in each whole? (Signal.) *5.*
- (Write to show:)

$$3\frac{2}{5} = \frac{15+2}{5} = \frac{17}{5}$$

- What fraction does 3 and 2 fifths equal? (Signal.) *17 fifths.*

EXERCISE 5

Multiplication/Addition/Subtraction

a. Touch the first problem in Part 3.
- The problems tell you to add or subtract or multiply. Skip the problems you can't do. In some problems, you'll have to change numbers to fractions before you multiply.

b. Work all of the problems in Part 3. You have 6 minutes.
- (Observe students and give feedback.)

EXERCISE 6

Workcheck

a. We're going to check the answers. Exchange workbooks, and get ready to check the answers. (Pause.)
- Put an **X** next to each problem that the person misses.
- (Check and correct. See **Answer Key.**)
- Return the workbooks.

b. Now we're going to figure out the number of points you've earned for this lesson.
- (Point to the posted information.)

Worksheet Items	Errors	Points
	0–2	10
	3	7
	4	5
	5	3
	6	1
	7 or more	0

- Count the number of items you got wrong. Figure out the number of points you earned and write the number in the "Items" box.
- (Observe students and give feedback.)

c. (Tell the group how many points they earned for the lesson.) Write that number in the "Hard Work" box; then figure out the total for today's lesson.

d. Turn to the Point Summary Charts. Write the points in the box for Lesson 45. ✔

e. Total your points for Lessons 41 through 45 and write the total number on the chart.
- (Observe students and give feedback.)

f. Everybody, find the Five-Lesson Point Graph. ✔
- (Help the students plot their five-lesson scores on the graph.)

EXERCISE 1

Multiplying by 1

a. Turn to Lesson 46.
- Touch the first problem in Part 1.
- You have to multiply by a fraction that equals 1 in these problems. Cross out the first fraction at the top of Part 1 that equals 1 and put it in the parentheses of the first problem. ✔
- When you multiply in that problem, what will the end amount equal? (Signal.) *4.*
- How do you know that it equals 4? (Signal.) *You're multiplying by 1.*

b. Work all of the problems in Part 1. Use a new fraction equal to 1 for each problem. Cross out a fraction as you use it. You have 2 minutes.
- (Observe students and give feedback.)

EXERCISE 2

Fractions to Wholes

a. Look at the problems in Part 2. You have to figure out the wholes that each fraction equals.

b. Touch the first fraction. What's the bottom number? (Signal.) *4.*
- Tell me how many times bigger than 4 is the top. Get ready. (Signal.) *2.*
- So how many wholes does the fraction equal? (Signal.) *2.*
- Write **equals 2.** ✔

c. Touch the next fraction. What's the bottom number? (Signal.) *8.*
- Tell me how many times bigger than 8 is the top? (Signal.) *4.*
- How many wholes does the fraction equal? (Signal.) *4.*
- Write **equals 4.** ✔

d. Work the rest of the problems in Part 2 the same way. You have 2 minutes.
- (Observe students and give feedback.)

EXERCISE 3

Expanding Fractions

a. (Write on the board:)

$$2\frac{2}{3} =$$

b. We're going to change this mixed number into a fraction.

- (Point to the $\frac{}{3}$.)
- The bottom number of the fraction tells us that we will have three parts in each whole. So I write a 3.
- (Write to show:)

$$2\frac{2}{3} = \frac{}{3}$$

- (Touch the first 2.)
- How many wholes do we have? (Signal.) *2.*
- A fraction equals 2 wholes when the top is 2 times bigger than the bottom. What's the bottom of the fraction we're writing? (Signal.) *3.*
- The top must be 2 times bigger than three. Tell me the number for the top. Get ready. (Signal.) *6.*
- (Write to show:)

$$2\frac{2}{3} = \frac{6}{3}$$

- We used the 2 wholes.
- (Touch the $\frac{2}{}$.)
- How many parts are left? (Signal.) *2.*
- (Write to show:)

$$2\frac{2}{3} = \frac{6 + 2}{3}$$

- We have 6 plus 2 parts. How many parts do we have altogether? (Signal.) *8.*

Lesson 46

- (Write to show:)

$$2\frac{2}{3} = \frac{6+2}{3} = \frac{8}{\boxed{}}$$

- How many parts are in each whole? (Signal.) *3.*
- (Write to show:)

$$2\frac{2}{3} = \frac{6+2}{3} = \frac{8}{3}$$

- What fraction does 2 and 2 thirds equal? (Signal.) *8 thirds.*

New Problem

a. (Write on the board:)

$$3\frac{4}{5} =$$

b. Let's change this mixed number into a fraction. How many parts will be in each whole? (Signal.) *5.*
- (Write to show:)

$$3\frac{4}{5} = \frac{}{5}$$

- How many wholes do we have? (Signal.) *3.*
- A fraction equals 3 wholes when the top is how many times bigger than the bottom? (Signal.) *3.*
- What's the bottom of the fraction we're writing? (Signal.) *5.*
- So the top must be 3 times bigger than 5. Tell me the number for the top. Get ready. (Signal.) *15.*
- (Write to show:)

$$3\frac{4}{5} = \frac{15}{5}$$

- We used 3 wholes. How many parts are left? (Signal.) *4.*
- (Write to show:)

$$3\frac{4}{5} = \frac{15+4}{5}$$

c. How many parts do we have altogether? (Signal.) *19.*
- (Write to show:)

$$3\frac{4}{5} = \frac{15+4}{5} = \frac{19}{\boxed{}}$$

- How many parts are in each whole? (Signal.) *5.*
- (Write to show:)

$$3\frac{4}{5} = \frac{15+4}{5} = \frac{19}{5}$$

- What fraction does 3 and 4 fifths equal? (Signal.) *19 fifths.*

New Problem

a. (Write on the board:)

$$6\frac{1}{3} =$$

b. Let's change this mixed number into a fraction. How many parts will be in each whole? (Signal.) *3.*
- (Write to show:)

$$6\frac{1}{3} = \frac{}{3}$$

- How many wholes do we have? (Signal.) *6.*
- A fraction equals 6 wholes when the top is how many times bigger than the bottom? (Signal.) *6.*
- What's the bottom of the fraction we're writing? (Signal.) *3.*
- So the top must be 6 times bigger than 3. Tell me the number for the top. Get ready. (Signal.) *18.*
- (Write to show:)

$$6\frac{1}{3} = \frac{18}{3}$$

- We used 6 wholes. How many parts are left? (Signal.) *1.*
- (Write to show:)

$$6\frac{1}{3} = \frac{18+1}{3}$$

c. How many parts do we have altogether? (Signal.) *19.*
- (Write to show:)

$$6\frac{1}{3} = \frac{18 + 1}{3}\ \boxed{\ \ }\ \frac{19}{\ \ }$$

- How many parts are in each whole? (Signal.) *3.*
- (Write to show:)

$$6\frac{1}{3} = \frac{18 + 1}{3} = \frac{19}{3}$$

- What fraction does 6 and 1 third equal? (Signal.) *19 thirds.*

EXERCISE 4

Multiplying by 1

a. Look at the problems in Part 3.
- You're going to multiply by 1 in these problems. First you have to write a fraction that equals 1 in the parentheses. Cross out the first fraction at the top of Part 3.
- What fraction will you use? (Signal.) *2 halves.*
- Write that fraction in the parentheses. There is no multiplication sign written in. The parentheses tell you to multiply. Now tell me what the amount you end with equals. (Signal.) *5.*
- How do you know it will equal 5? (Signal.) *You're multiplying by 1.*
- Figure out the answer when you multiply. (Pause).
- What's the answer? (Signal.) *10 halves.*
- If 10 halves equals 5, the top number must be 5 times bigger than the bottom number. Tell me how many times bigger than 2 is 10. Get ready. (Signal.) *5.*

- So what does 10 halves equal? (Signal.) *5.*
- Write **equals 5** following the fraction.
b. Touch the next problem.
- Cross out the next fraction that equals 1 and put it in the parentheses. Remember, the parentheses tell you to multiply. Tell me what the amount you end with equals. (Signal.) *2.*
- How do you know it will equal 2? (Signal.) *You're multiplying by 1.*
- Figure out the answer when you multiply. (Pause.)
- What's the answer? (Signal.) *8 fourths.*
- If 8 fourths equals 2, the top number must be 2 times bigger than the bottom number. Tell me how many times bigger than 4 is 8. Get ready. (Signal.) *2.*
- So what does 8 fourths equal? (Signal.) *2.*
- Write **equals 2** following the fraction. ✔
c. Work the rest of the problems in Part 3. Use a new fraction that equals 1 each time. Remember to write how many wholes your answer equals. You have 2 minutes.
- (Observe students and give feedback.)

EXERCISE 5

Multiplication/Addition/ Subtraction

a. Look at the problems in Part 4.
- The problems tell you to add or subtract or multiply. Skip the problems you can't do. In some problems, you'll have to change numbers to fractions before you multiply.
b. Work all of the problems in Part 4. You have 4 minutes.
- (Observe students and give feedback.)

EXERCISE 6

Workcheck

a. We're going to check the answers. Exchange workbooks, and get ready to check the answers. (Pause.)

- Put an **X** next to each problem that the person misses.
- (Check and correct. See **Answer Key.**)
- Return the workbooks.

b. Now we're going to figure out the number of points you've earned for this lesson.

- (Point to the posted information.)

Worksheet Items	Errors	Points
	0–2	10
	3	7
	4	5
	5	3
	6	1
	7 or more	0

- Count the number of items you got wrong. Figure out the number of points you earned and write the number in the "Items" box.
- (Observe students and give feedback.)

c. (Tell the group how many points they earned for the lesson.) Write that number in the "Hard Work" box; then figure out the total for today's lesson.

d. Turn to the Point Summary Charts. Write the points in the box for Lesson 46. ✔

Lesson 47

EXERCISE 1
Multiplying by 1

a. Turn to Lesson 47.
- Look at the problems in Part 1.
- You're going to multiply by 1 in these problems. First you have to write a fraction that equals 1 in the parentheses. Cross out the first fraction that equals 1 at the top of Part 1. What fraction will you use? (Signal.) *3 thirds.*
- Write that fraction in the parentheses. There is no multiplication sign. The parentheses tell you to multiply. Now tell me what the amount you end with equals. (Signal.) *5.*
- How do you know it will equal 5? (Signal.) *You're multiplying by 1.*
- Figure out the answer when you multiply. (Pause.)
- What's the answer? (Signal.) *15 thirds.*
- If 15 thirds equals 5, the top number must be 5 times bigger than the bottom number.
- Tell me how many times bigger than 3 is 15. Get ready. (Signal.) *5.*
- So what does 15 thirds equal? (Signal.) *5.*
- Write **equals 5** following the fraction. ✔

b. Touch the next problem.
- Cross out the next fraction that equals 1 and put it in the parentheses. Remember, the parentheses tell you to multiply.
- Tell me what will the amount you end with equal? (Signal.) *7.*
- How do you know it will equal 7? (Signal.) *You're multiplying by 1.*
- Figure out the answer when you multiply. (Pause.)
- What's the answer? (Signal.) *42 sixths.*
- If 42 sixths equals 7, the top number must be 7 times bigger than the bottom number.
- Tell me how many times bigger than 6 is 42. Get ready. (Signal.) *7.*
- So what does 42 sixths equal? (Signal.) *7.*
- Write **equals 7** following the fraction. ✔

c. Work the rest of the problems in Part 1. Use a new fraction that equals 1 each time.

Remember to write how many wholes your answer equals. You have 2 minutes.
- (Observe students and give feedback.)

EXERCISE 2
Generating Series

a. I'm going to give you clues about different fractions that are equal to 1. See whether you can figure out each fraction.

b. This fraction equals 1 and the bottom number is 6. Tell me the fraction equal to 1. (Signal.) *6 sixths.*

c. This fraction equals 1 and the top number is 2. Tell me the fraction equal to 1. (Signal.) *2 halves.*

d. This fraction equals 1 and the top number is 12. Tell me the fraction equal to 1. (Signal.) *12 twelfths.*

e. This fraction equals 1 and the bottom number is 9. Tell me the fraction equal to 1. (Signal.) *9 ninths.*

f. This fraction equals 1 and the top number is 5. Tell me the fraction equal to 1. (Signal.) *5 fifths.*

g. This fraction equals 1 and the bottom number is 4. Tell me the fraction equal to 1. (Signal.) *4 fourths.*

h. This fraction equals 1 and the bottom number is 10. Tell me the fraction equal to 1. (Signal.) *10 tenths.*

EXERCISE 3
Multiplication/Addition/ Subtraction

a. Look at the problems in Part 2. The problems tell you to add or subtract or multiply. Skip the problems you can't do. In some problems, you'll have to change numbers to fractions before you multiply.

b. Work all of the problems in Part 2. You have 3 minutes.
- (Observe students and give feedback.)

EXERCISE 4

Expanding Fractions

a. (Write on the board:)

$$2\frac{5}{7} =$$

- Let's change this mixed number into a fraction. How many parts will be in each whole? (Signal.) *7.*
- (Write to show:)

$$2\frac{5}{7} = \frac{}{7}$$

- How many wholes do we have? (Signal.) *2.*
- A fraction equals 2 wholes when the top is how many times bigger than the bottom? (Signal.) *2.*
- What's the bottom of the fraction we're writing? (Signal.) *7.*
- So the top must be 2 times bigger than 7. Tell me the number for the top. Get ready. (Signal.) *14.*
- (Write to show:)

$$2\frac{5}{7} = \frac{14}{7}$$

- We used the 2 wholes. How many parts are left? (Signal.) *5.*
- (Write to show:)

$$2\frac{5}{7} = \frac{14 + 5}{7}$$

- How many parts do we have altogether? (Signal.) *19.*
- (Write to show:)

$$2\frac{5}{7} = \frac{14 + 5}{7} = \frac{19}{}$$

- How many parts are in each whole? (Signal.) *7.*
- (Write to show:)

$$2\frac{5}{7} = \frac{14 + 5}{7} = \frac{19}{7}$$

- What fraction does 2 and 5 sevenths equal? (Signal.) *19 sevenths.*

b. (Write on the board:)

$$1\frac{5}{8} =$$

- Let's change this mixed number into a fraction. How many parts will be in each whole? (Signal.) *8.*
- (Write to show:)

$$1\frac{5}{8} = \frac{}{8}$$

- How many wholes do we have? (Signal.) *1.*
- A fraction equals 1 whole when the top is the same as the bottom. What's the bottom of the fraction we are writing? (Signal.) *8.*
- So tell me the number for the top. Get ready. (Signal.) *8.*
- (Write to show:)

$$1\frac{5}{8} = \frac{8}{8}$$

- We used 1 whole. How many parts are left? (Signal.) *5.*
- (Write to show:)

$$1\frac{5}{8} = \frac{8 + 5}{8}$$

- How many parts do we have altogether? (Signal.) *13.*
- (Write to show:)

$$1\frac{5}{8} = \frac{8 + 5}{8} = \frac{13}{}$$

- How many parts are in each whole? (Signal.) *8.*
- (Write to show:)

$$1\frac{5}{8} = \frac{8 + 5}{8} = \frac{13}{8}$$

- What fraction does 1 and 5 eighths equal? (Signal.) *13 eighths.*

EXERCISE 5

Expanding Fractions

a. Touch the first problem in Part 3.
- You have to change the mixed number into a fraction. How many parts are going to be in each whole? (Signal.) *4.*
- Write that. ✔
- How many wholes do you have? (Signal.) *3.*
- That means the top will be how many times bigger than the bottom? (Signal.) *3.*
- Tell me the number for the top that is 3 times bigger than the bottom. Get ready. (Signal.) *12.*
- Write that on top. ✔
- You used the 3 wholes. How many parts are left? (Signal.) *1.*
- Write that. ✔
- Tell me how many parts you have altogether. Get ready. (Signal.) *13.*
- Write the numbers for the top and the bottom. ✔
- What fraction does 3 and 1 fourth equal? (Signal.) *13 fourths.*

b. Touch the next problem.
- How many parts will be in each whole? (Signal.) *5.*
- Write that. ✔
- How many wholes do you have? (Signal.) *2.*
- That means the top will be how many times bigger than the bottom? (Signal.) *2.*
- Tell me the number for the top. Get ready. (Signal.) *10.*
- Write that on top. ✔
- You used the 2 wholes. How many parts are left? (Signal.) *4.*
- Write that. ✔
- How many parts do you have altogether? (Signal.) *14.*
- Write the numbers for the top and the bottom. ✔
- What fraction does 2 and 4 fifths equal? (Signal.) *14 fifths.*

c. Touch the next problem.
- How many parts will be in each whole? (Signal.) *8.*
- Write that. ✔
- How many wholes do you have? (Signal.) *1.*

- A fraction equals 1 when the top is the same as the bottom.
- Tell me the number for the top. Get ready. (Signal.) *8.*
- Write that on top. ✔
- You used the 1 whole. How many parts are left? (Signal.) *7.*
- Write that. ✔
- How many parts do you have altogether? (Signal.) *15.*
- Write the numbers for the top and the bottom. ✔
- What fraction does 1 and 7 eighths equal? (Signal.) *15 eighths.*

d. Work the rest of the problems in Part 3. You have 5 minutes.
- (Observe students and give feedback.)

EXERCISE 6

Workcheck

a. We're going to check the answers. Exchange workbooks, and get ready to check the answers. (Pause.)
- Put an **X** next to each problem that the person misses.
- (Check and correct. See **Answer Key**.)
- Return the workbooks.

b. Now we're going to figure out the number of points you've earned for this lesson.
- (Point to the posted information.)

Worksheet Items	Errors	Points
	0–2	10
	3	7
	4	5
	5	3
	6	1
	7 or more	0

- Count the number of items you got wrong. Figure out the number of points you earned and write the number in the "Items" box.
- (Observe students and give feedback.)

c. (Tell the group how many points they earned for the lesson.) Write that number in the "Hard Work" box; then figure out the total for today's lesson.

d. Turn to the Point Summary Charts. Write the points in the box for Lesson 47. ✔

EXERCISE 1

Multiplication/Addition/ Subtraction

a. Turn to Lesson 48.
• Look at the problems in Part 1.
• The problems tell you to add or subtract or multiply. Skip the problems you can't do. In some problems, you'll have to change numbers to fractions before you multiply.

b. Work all of the problems in Part 1. You have 4 minutes.
• (Observe students and give feedback.)

EXERCISE 2

Expanding Fractions

a. Touch the first problem in Part 2.
• You have to change the mixed number into a fraction. How many parts are going to be in each whole? (Signal.) *4.*
• Write that. ✔
• How many wholes do you have? (Signal.) *2.*
• That means the top will be how many times bigger than the bottom? (Signal.) *2.*
• Tell me the number for the top. Get ready. (Signal.) *8.*
• Write that on top. ✔
• You used the 2 wholes. How many parts are left? (Signal.) *3.*
• Write that. ✔
• How many parts do you have altogether? (Signal.) *11.*
• Write the numbers for the top and the bottom. ✔
• What fraction does 2 and 3 fourths equal? (Signal.) *11 fourths.*

b. Touch the next problem.
• How many parts will be in each whole? (Signal.) *3.*
• Write that. ✔
• How many wholes do you have? (Signal.) *1.*
• A fraction equals 1 when the top is the same as the bottom.
• Tell me the number for the top. Get ready. (Signal.) *3.*

• Write that on top. ✔
• You used 1 whole. How many parts are left? (Signal.) *2.*
• Write that. ✔
• Tell me how many parts you have altogether. Get ready. (Signal.) *5.*
• Write the numbers for the top and the bottom. ✔
• What fraction does one and 2 thirds equal? (Signal.) *5 thirds.*

c. Do the rest of the problems in Part 2. You have 3 minutes.
• (Observe students and give feedback.)

EXERCISE 3

Multiplying by 1

a. Look at the problems in Part 3.
• You're going to multiply by 1 in these problems. First you have to write a fraction that equals 1. Cross out the first fraction that equals 1 at the top of Part 3. What fraction will you use? (Signal.) *5 fifths.*
• Write that fraction in the parentheses. The parentheses tell you to multiply. Now tell me what the amount you end with equals. (Signal.) *7.*
• How do you know it will equal 7? (Signal.) *You're multiplying by 1.*
• Figure out the answer when you multiply. (Pause.)
• What's the answer? (Signal.) *35 fifths.*
• If 35 fifths equals 7, the top number must be 7 times bigger than the bottom number. Tell me how many times bigger than 5 is 35. Get ready. (Signal.) *7.*
• So what does 35 fifths equal? (Signal.) *7.*
• Write **equals 7** following the fraction. ✔

b. Touch the next problem.
• Cross out the next fraction equal to 1 and put it in the parentheses. Remember, the parentheses tell you to multiply. Tell me what the amount you end with equals. (Signal.) *6.*
• How do you know it will equal 6? (Signal.) *You're multiplying by 1.*

- Figure out the answer when you multiply. (Pause.)
- What's the answer? (Signal.) *24 fourths.*
- If 24 fourths equals 6, the top number must be 6 times bigger than the bottom number. How many times bigger than 4 is 24? (Pause. Signal.) *6.*
- So what does 24 fourths equal? (Signal.) *6.*
- Write **equals 6** following the fraction. ✔

c. Work the rest of the problems in Part 3. Use a new fraction that equals 1 each time. Remember to write how many wholes your answer equals. You have 3 minutes.
- (Observe students and give feedback.)

EXERCISE 4

Generating Series

a. I'm going to give you clues about different fractions that are equal to 1. See whether you can figure out each fraction.

b. This fraction equals 1 and the bottom number is 6. Tell me the fraction equal to 1. (Signal.) *6 sixths.*

c. This fraction equals 1 and the top number is 3. Tell me the fraction equal to 1. (Signal.) *3 thirds.*

d. This fraction equals 1 and the top number is 5. Tell me the fraction equal to 1. (Signal.) *5 fifths.*

e. This fraction equals 1 and the bottom number is 7. Tell me the fraction equal to 1. (Signal.) *7 sevenths.*

EXERCISE 5

Generating Series

a. (Write on the board:)

$$\frac{2}{3}\left(\frac{-}{-}\right) = \frac{-}{6}$$

- In this problem, we are multiplying by a fraction that equals 1. We have to figure out the fraction that equals 1 to put in the parentheses.

- (Touch $\frac{2}{3}$.)
- What's the bottom number we start with? (Signal.) *3.*
- (Touch $\frac{-}{6}$.)
- What's the bottom number we end with? (Signal.) *6.*
- (Touch $\frac{-}{3}$.)
- Tell me 3 times how many (touch $\left(\frac{-}{-}\right)$) equals 6 (touch $\frac{-}{6}$.). Get ready. (Signal.) *2.*
- That's the bottom number.
- (Write to show:)

$$\frac{2}{3}\left(\frac{-}{2}\right) = \frac{-}{6}$$

- (Touch $\frac{-}{2}$.)
- The fraction in parentheses equals 1, so what does the top have to be? (Signal.) *2.*
- (Write to show:)

$$\frac{2}{3}\left(\frac{2}{2}\right) = \frac{-}{6}$$

- You figured out the fraction equal to 1 to use.

b. (Write on the board:)

$$\frac{7}{2}\left(\frac{-}{-}\right) = \frac{-}{8}$$

- Let's figure out the fraction that equals 1 to put in the parentheses.
- What's the bottom number we start with? (Signal.) *2.*
- What's the bottom number we end with? (Signal.) *8.*
- Tell me 2 times how many equals 8. Get ready. (Signal.) *4.*

- That's the bottom number.
- (Write to show:)

$$\frac{7}{2}\left(\frac{}{4}\right) = \frac{}{8}$$

- The fraction in parentheses equals 1, so what does the top have to be? (Signal.) *4.*
- (Write to show:)

$$\frac{7}{2}\left(\frac{4}{4}\right) = \frac{}{8}$$

- You figured out the fraction equal to 1 to use.

c. (Write on the board:)

$$\frac{5}{4}\left(\frac{}{}\right) = \frac{}{24}$$

- Let's figure out the fraction that equals 1 in the next problem.
- What's the bottom number we start with? (Signal.) *4.*
- What's the bottom number we end with? (Signal.) *24.*
- Tell me 4 times how many equals 24. Get ready. (Signal.) *6.*
- That's the bottom number.
- (Write to show:)

$$\frac{5}{4}\left(\frac{}{6}\right) = \frac{}{24}$$

- The fraction in parentheses equals 1, so what does the top have to be? (Signal.) *6.*
- (Write to show:)

$$\frac{5}{4}\left(\frac{6}{6}\right) = \frac{}{24}$$

- You figured out the fraction equal to 1 to use.

EXERCISE 6

Workcheck

a. We're going to check the answers. Exchange workbooks, and get ready to check the answers. (Pause.)
- Put an **X** next to each problem that the person misses.
- (Check and correct. See ***Answer Key.***)
- Return the workbooks.
b. Now we're going to figure out the number of points you've earned for this lesson.
- (Point to the posted information.)

Worksheet Items	Errors	Points
	0–2	10
	3	7
	4	5
	5	3
	6	1
	7 or more	0

- Count the number of items you got wrong. Figure out the number of points you earned and write the number in the "Items" box.
- (Observe students and give feedback.)
c. (Tell the group how many points they earned for the lesson.) Write that number in the "Hard Work" box; then figure out the total for today's lesson.
d. Turn to the Point Summary Charts. Write the points in the box for Lesson 48. ✔

Lesson 49

Skipping Note: Check the students' errors from Lesson 48. If no more than 1 fourth of the students made more than 4 errors, skip this lesson and proceed with Lesson 50.

EXERCISE 1
Expanding Fractions

a. Turn to Lesson 49.
- Touch the first problem in Part 1.
- You have to change the mixed number into a fraction. How many parts are going to be in each whole? (Signal.) *5.*
- Write the line and the bottom number.
- How many wholes do you have? (Signal.) *3.*
- That means the top will be how many times bigger than the bottom? (Signal.) *3.*
- Tell me the number for the top. Get ready. (Signal.) *15.*
- Write that on top. ✔
- You used the 3 wholes. How many parts are left? (Signal.) *3.*
- Write that. ✔
- Tell me how many parts you have altogether. Get ready. (Signal.) *18.*
- Write the numbers for the top and the bottom. ✔
- What fraction does 3 and 3 fifths equal? (Signal.) *18 fifths.*

b. Touch the next problem.
- How many parts will be in each whole? (Signal.) *3.*
- Write the line and the bottom number. ✔
- How many wholes do you have? (Signal.) *2.*
- That means the top will be how many times bigger than the bottom? (Signal.) *2.*
- Tell me the number for the top. Get ready. (Signal.) *6.*
- Write that on top. ✔
- You used the 2 wholes. How many parts are left? (Signal.) *1.*
- Tell me how many parts you have altogether. Get ready. (Signal.) *7.*

- Write the numbers for the top and the bottom. ✔
- What fraction does 2 and 1 third equal? (Signal.) *7 thirds.*

c. Do the rest of the problems in Part 1. You have 3 minutes.
- (Observe students and give feedback.)

EXERCISE 2
Multiplying by 1

a. Look at the problems in Part 2.
- You're going to multiply by 1 in these problems. Cross out the first fraction that equals 1 at the top of Part 2. What fraction equal to 1 will you use? (Signal.) *4 fourths.*
- Write the fraction in the parentheses. The parentheses tell you to multiply.
- Now tell me what the amount you end with equals. (Signal.) *7.*
- How do you know it will equal 7? (Signal.) *You're multiplying by 1.*
- Figure out the answer when you multiply. (Pause.)
- What's the answer? (Signal.) *28 fourths.*
- If 28 fourths equals 7, the top number must be 7 times bigger than the bottom number.
- Tell me how many times bigger than 4 is 28. Get ready. (Signal.) *7.*
- So what does 28 fourths equal? (Signal.) *7.*
- Write **equals 7** following the fraction. ✔

b. Touch the next problem.
- Cross out the next fraction equal to 1 and put it in the parentheses. Remember, the parentheses tell you to multiply. Tell me what the amount you end with equals. (Signal.) *2.*
- How do you know it will equal 2? (Signal.) *You're multiplying by 1.*
- Figure out the answer when you multiply. (Pause.)
- What's the answer? (Signal.) *8 fourths.*
- If 8 fourths equals 2, the top number must be 2 times bigger than the bottom number.
- Tell me how many times bigger than 4 is 8. Get ready. (Signal.) *2.*

- So what does 8 fourths equal? (Signal.) *2.*
- Write **equals 2** following the fraction. ✔
c. Work the rest of the problems in Part 2. Use a new fraction that equals 1 each time. Remember to write how many wholes your answer equals. You have 3 minutes.
- (Observe students and give feedback.)

EXERCISE 3

Generating Series

a. (Write on the board:)

$$\frac{3}{7}\left(-\right) = \frac{}{14}$$

- In this problem, we are multiplying by a fraction that equals 1. We have to figure out the fraction that equals 1 to put in the parentheses.
- (Touch $\frac{3}{7}$.)
- What's the bottom number we start with? (Signal.) *7.*
- (Touch $\frac{}{14}$.)
- What's the bottom number we end with? (Signal.) *14.*
- (Touch $\frac{}{7}$.)
- Tell me 7 times how many (touch $\left(-\right)$)

  equals 14 (touch $\frac{}{14}$). Get ready. (Signal.) *2.*
- That's the bottom number.
- (Write to show:)

$$\frac{3}{7}\left(\frac{}{2}\right) = \frac{}{14}$$

- (Touch $\frac{}{2}$.)

- The fraction in parentheses equals 1, so what does the top have to be? (Signal.) *2.*
- (Write to show:)

$$\frac{3}{7}\left(\frac{2}{2}\right) = \frac{}{14}$$

- You figured out the fraction equal to 1 to use.
b. (Write on the board:)

$$\frac{8}{3}\left(-\right) = \frac{}{12}$$

- Let's figure out the fraction that equals 1 to put in the parentheses.
- What's the bottom number we start with? (Signal.) *3.*
- What's the bottom number we end with? (Signal.) *12.*
- Tell me 3 times how many equals 12. (Pause. Signal.) *4.*
- That's the bottom number.
- (Write to show:)

$$\frac{8}{3}\left(\frac{}{4}\right) = \frac{}{12}$$

- The fraction in parentheses equals 1, so what does the top have to be? (Signal.) *4.*
- (Write to show:)

$$\frac{8}{3}\left(\frac{4}{4}\right) = \frac{}{12}$$

- You figured out the fraction equal to 1 to use.

EXERCISE 4

Multiplication/Addition/Subtraction

a. Look at the problems in Part 3.
- The problems tell you to add or subtract or multiply. Skip the problems you can't do. In some problems, you'll have to change numbers to fractions before you multiply.

b. Work all of the problems in Part 3. You have 4 minutes.
- (Observe students and give feedback.)

EXERCISE 5
Workcheck

a. We're going to check the answers. Exchange workbooks, and get ready to check the answers. (Pause.)
- Put an **X** next to each problem that the person misses.
- (Check and correct. See **Answer Key.**)
- Return the workbooks.

b. Now we're going to figure out the number of points you've earned for this lesson.
- (Point to the posted information.)

Worksheet Items	Errors	Points
	0–2	10
	3	7
	4	5
	5	3
	6	1
	7 or more	0

- Count the number of items you got wrong. Figure out the number of points you earned and write the number in the "Items" box.
- (Observe students and give feedback.)

c. (Tell the group how many points they earned for the lesson.) Write that number in the "Hard Work" box; then figure out the total for today's lesson.

d. Turn to the Point Summary Charts. Write the points in the box for Lesson 49. ✔

Lesson 50

EXERCISE 1

Generating Series

a. (Write on the board:)

$$\frac{4}{5}\left(\frac{}{}\right)=\frac{}{15}$$

- In this problem, we are multiplying by a fraction that equals 1. We have to figure out the fraction that equals 1 to put in the parentheses.
- What's the bottom number we start with? (Signal.) *5.*
- What's the bottom number we end with? (Signal.) *15.*
- Tell me 5 times how many equals 15. Get ready. (Signal.) *3.*
- That's the bottom number.
- (Write to show:)

$$\frac{4}{5}\left(\frac{}{3}\right)=\frac{}{15}$$

- The fraction in parentheses equals 1, so what does the top have to be? (Signal.) *3.*
- (Write to show:)

$$\frac{4}{5}\left(\frac{3}{3}\right)=\frac{}{15}$$

- You figured out the fraction equal to 1 to use.

EXERCISE 2

Multiplying by 1

a. Turn to Lesson 50.
- Look at the problems in Part 1.
- You're going to multiply by 1. You have to figure out the fraction equal to 1 that goes in the parentheses. These are easy because the bottom number is 1.
b. Touch the first problem.
- What's the bottom number you start with? (Signal.) *1.*

- What's the bottom number you end with? (Signal.) *5.*
- What do you have to multiply 1 by to end with 5? (Signal.) *5.*
- Tell me the whole fraction equal to 1 that goes in the parentheses. (Signal.) *5 fifths.*
- Write it. Then figure out the answer when you multiply. (Pause.)
- What's the answer? (Signal.) *20 fifths.*
- If 20 fifths equals 4, the top number must be 4 times bigger than the bottom number.
- Tell me how many times bigger than 5 is 20. Get ready. (Signal.) *4.*
- So how many wholes does 20 fifths equal? (Signal.) *4.*
- Write **equals 4**.
c. Touch the next problem.
- What's the bottom number you start with? (Signal.) *1.*
- What's the bottom number you end with? (Signal.) *7.*
- What do you have to multiply 1 by to end with 7? (Signal.) *7.*
- Tell me the whole fraction equal to 1 that goes in the parentheses. (Signal.) *7 sevenths.*
- Write it. Then figure out the answer when you multiply. (Pause.)
- What's the answer? (Signal.) *35 sevenths.*
- If 35 sevenths equals 5, the top number must be 5 times bigger than the bottom number.
- Tell me how many times bigger than 7 is 35. Get ready. (Signal.) *5.*
- So how many wholes does 35 sevenths equal? (Signal.) *5.*
- Write **equals 5** following the fraction. ✔
d. Touch the next problem.
- What's the bottom number you start with? (Signal.) *1.*
- What's the bottom number you end with? (Signal.) *9.*
- What do you have to multiply 1 by to end with 9? (Signal.) *9.*
- Tell me the whole fraction equal to 1 that goes in the parentheses. (Signal.) *9 ninths.*
- Write it. Then figure out the answer when you multiply. (Pause.)

- What's the answer? (Signal.) *18 ninths.*
- If 18 ninths equals 2, the top number must be 2 times bigger than the bottom number.
- Tell me how many times bigger than 9 is 18. Get ready. (Signal.) *2.*
- So how many wholes does 18 ninths equal? (Signal.) *2.*
- Write **equals 2** following the fraction.

e. Work the rest of the problems in Part 1. Figure out the fraction equal to 1 that goes in the parentheses. Then work the problem, and write how many wholes the fraction equals. You have 2 minutes.

- (Observe students and give feedback.)

EXERCISE 3

Expanding Fractions

a. Touch the first problem in Part 2.
- You have to change the mixed number into a fraction. How many parts are going to be in each whole? (Signal.) *5.* ✔
- Write the line and the bottom number. ✔
- How many wholes do you have? (Signal.) *2.*
- That means the top will be how many times bigger than the bottom? (Signal.) *2.*
- Tell me the number for the top. Get ready. (Signal.) *10.*
- Write that on top. ✔
- You used the 2 wholes. How many parts are left? (Signal.) *1.*
- Write it. ✔
- Tell me how many parts you have altogether. Get ready. (Signal.) *11.*
- Write numbers for the top and the bottom. ✔
- What fraction does 2 and 1 fifth equal? (Signal.) *11 fifths.*

b. Work all of the problems in Part 2. You have 3 minutes.
- (Observe students and give feedback.)

EXERCISE 4

Expanding Fractions

a. Touch the first problem in Part 3.
- You have to write that mixed number as a fraction. Write the number of parts that will be in each whole.
- How many wholes do you have? (Signal.) *2.*
- So the top will be how many times bigger than the bottom? (Signal.) *2.*
- Write the number on top for the wholes, and then write in the number of parts that are left.
- Figure out the fraction. (Pause.)
- What's the fraction? (Signal.) *17 sevenths.*

b. Touch the next problem.
- You have to write that mixed number as a fraction. Write the number of parts that will be in each whole. ✔
- How many wholes do you have? (Signal.) *3.*
- So the top will be how many times bigger than the bottom? (Signal.) *3.*
- Write the number on top for the wholes, and then write in the number of parts that are left.
- Figure out the fraction. (Pause.)
- What's the fraction? (Signal.) *13 fourths.*

c. Touch the next problem.
- There is a number. You have to write that number as a fraction.
- What will you write? (Signal.) *9 over 1.*
- Write it. ✔

d. Touch the next problem.
- There is a fraction, so you have to write it as a number.
- What's the bottom number? (Signal.) *9.*
- Tell me how many times bigger than 9 is the top. Get ready. (Signal.) *2.*
- So what number does the fraction equal? (Signal.) *2.*
- Write it. ✔

e. Do the rest of the problems in Part 3. Write a number for each fraction. Write a fraction for each number and each mixed number. You have 3 minutes.

- (Observe students and give feedback.)

Lesson 50

EXERCISE 5

Multiplication/Addition/Subtraction

a. Look at the problems in Part 4. The problems tell you to add or subtract or multiply. Skip the problems you can't do. In some problems, you'll have to change numbers to fractions before you multiply.

b. Work all of the problems in Part 4. You have 2 minutes.

- (Observe students and give feedback.)

EXERCISE 6

Workcheck

a. We're going to check the answers. Exchange workbooks, and get ready to check the answers. (Pause.)

- Put an **X** next to each problem that the person misses.
- (Check and correct. See **Answer Key.**)
- Return the workbooks.

b. Now we're going to figure out the number of points you've earned for this lesson.

- (Point to the posted information.)

Worksheet Items	Errors	Points
	0–2	10
	3	7
	4	5
	5	3
	6	1
	7 or more	0

- Count the number of items you got wrong. Figure out the number of points you earned and write the number in the "Items" box.
- (Observe students and give feedback.)

c. (Tell the group how many points they earned for the lesson.) Write that number in the "Hard Work" box; then figure out the total for today's lesson.

d. Turn to the Point Summary Charts. Write the points in the box for Lesson 50. ✔

e. Total your points for Lessons 46 through 50 and write the total number on the chart.

- (Observe students and give feedback.)

f. Everybody, find the Five-Lesson Point Graph. ✔

- (Help the students plot their five-lesson scores on the graph.)

Lesson 51

EXERCISE 1

Multiplying by 1

a. Turn to Lesson 51.
  - Look at the problems in Part 1. You're going to multiply by 1.
  - You have to figure out the fraction equal to 1 that goes in the parentheses. In each of these problems, we start with 1 as the bottom number.

b. Touch the first problem.
  - What's the bottom number you start with? (Signal.) *1.*
  - What's the bottom number you end with? (Signal.) *7.*
  - What do you have to multiply 1 by to end with 7? (Signal.) *7.*
  - Tell me the whole fraction equal to 1 that goes in the parentheses. (Signal.) *7 sevenths.*
  - Write it. Then figure out the answer when you multiply. (Pause.)
  - What's the answer? (Signal.) *35 sevenths.*
  - If 35 sevenths equals 5, the top number must be 5 times bigger than the bottom number. Tell me how many times bigger than 7 is 35. Get ready. (Signal.) *5.*
  - So how many wholes does 35 sevenths equal? (Signal.) *5.*
  - Write **equals 5.** ✔

c. Touch the next problem.
  - What's the bottom number you start with? (Signal.) *1.*
  - What's the bottom number you end with? (Signal.) *10.*
  - What do you have to multiply 1 by to end with 10? (Signal.) *10.*
  - Tell me the whole fraction equal to 1 that goes in the parentheses. (Signal.) *10 tenths.*
  - Write it. Then figure out the answer when you multiply. (Pause.)
  - What's the answer? (Signal.) *20 tenths.*
  - If 20 tenths equals 2, the top number must be 2 times bigger than the bottom number.
  - Tell me how many times bigger than 10 is 20. Get ready. (Signal.) *2.*

  - How many wholes does 20 tenths equal? (Signal.) *2.*
  - Write **equals 2.** ✔

d. Work the rest of the problems in Part 1. Figure out the fraction equal to 1 that goes in the parentheses. Then work the problem, and write how many wholes the fraction equals. You have 2 minutes.
  - (Observe students and give feedback.)

EXERCISE 2

Multiplication/Addition/ Subtraction

a. Look at the problems in Part 2.
  - The problems tell you to add or subtract or multiply. Skip the problems you can't do. In some problems, you'll have to change numbers to fractions before you multiply.

b. Work all of the problems in Part 2. You have 4 minutes.
  - (Observe students and give feedback.)

EXERCISE 3

Expanding Fractions

a. Touch the first problem in Part 3
  - You have to change the mixed number into a fraction. Write the number of parts that will be in each whole.
  - How many wholes do you have? (Signal.) *3.*
  - So the top will be how many times bigger than the bottom? (Signal.) *3.*
  - Write that on top for the wholes, and then write in the number of parts that are left.
  - Figure out the fraction. (Pause.)
  - What's the fraction? (Signal.) *15 fourths.*

b. Touch the next problem.
  - There is a number you have to write as a fraction.
  - What will you write? (Signal.) *8 over 1.*
  - Write it.

c. Touch the next problem.
  - There is a fraction you have to write as a number.
  - What's the bottom number? (Signal.) *4.*

- How many times bigger than 4 is the top? (Signal.) *3.*
- Write it.
d. Touch the next problem.
- You have to write the mixed number as a fraction. Write the number of parts that will be in each whole.
- How many wholes do you have? (Signal.) *4.*
- So the top will be how many times bigger than the bottom? (Signal.) *4.*
- Write that on top for the wholes, and then write in the number of parts that are left. ✔
- Figure out the fraction. (Pause.)
- What's the fraction? (Signal.) *13 thirds.*
e. Do the rest of the problems in Part 3. Write a number for each fraction. Write a fraction for each number and each mixed number. You have 4 minutes.
- (Observe students and give feedback.)

EXERCISE 4

Workcheck

a. We're going to check the answers. Exchange workbooks, and get ready to check the answers. (Pause.)
- Put an **X** next to each problem that the person misses.
- (Check and correct. See **Answer Key.**)
- Return the workbooks.

b. Now we're going to figure out the number of points you've earned for this lesson.
- (Point to the posted information.)

Worksheet Items	Errors	Points
	0–2	10
	3	7
	4	5
	5	3
	6	1
	7 or more	0

- Count the number of items you got wrong. Figure out the number of points you earned and write the number in the "Items" box.
- (Observe students and give feedback.)
c. (Tell the group how many points they earned for the lesson.) Write that number in the "Hard Work" box; then figure out the total for today's lesson.
d. Turn to the Point Summary Charts. Write the points in the box for Lesson 51. ✔

EXERCISE 1

Multiplying by 1

a. Turn to Lesson 52.
- Look at the problems in Part 1.
- You're going to multiply by 1. You have to figure out the fraction equal to 1 that goes in the parentheses.

b. Touch the first problem.
- What's the bottom number you start with? (Signal.) *1.*
- What's the bottom number you end with? (Signal.) *5.*
- What do you have to multiply 1 by to end with 5? (Signal.) *5.*
- Tell me the whole fraction equal to 1 that goes in the parentheses. (Signal.) *5 fifths.*
- Write it. Then figure out the answer when you multiply. (Pause.)
- What's the answer? (Signal.) *30 fifths.*
- If 30 fifths equals 6, the top number must be 6 times bigger than the bottom number.
- Tell me how many times bigger than 5 is 30. Get ready. (Signal.) *6.*
- So how many wholes does 30 fifths equal? (Signal.) *6.*
- Write **equals 6.** ✔

c. Work the rest of the problems in Part 1. Figure out the fraction equal to 1 that goes in the parentheses. Then work the problem, and write how many wholes the fraction equals. You have 2 minutes.
- (Observe students and give feedback.)

EXERCISE 2

Expanding Fractions

a. Touch the first problem in Part 2.
- You have to change the mixed number into a fraction. Write the number of parts that will be in each whole. ✔
- How many wholes do you have? (Signal.) *4.*
- So the top will be how many times bigger than the bottom? (Signal.) *4.*
- Write the number on top for the wholes, and then write in the number of parts that are left.

- Figure out the fraction. (Pause.)
- What's the fraction? (Signal.) *17 fourths.*

b. Touch the next problem.
- There is a fraction you have to write as a number.
- What's the bottom number? (Signal.) *5.*
- Tell me how many times bigger than 5 is the top. Get ready. (Signal.) *8.*
- So what number does the fraction equal? (Signal.) *8.*
- Write it. ✔

c. Touch the next problem.
- There is a number you have to write as a fraction.
- What will you write? (Signal.) *8 over 1.*
- Write it.

d. Touch the next problem.
- There is a fraction you have to write as a number.
- What's the bottom number? (Signal.) *2.*
- How many times bigger than 2 is the top? (Signal.) *5.*
- Write it.

e. Do the rest of the problems in Part 2. Write a number for each fraction. Write a fraction for each number and each mixed number. You have 2 minutes.
- (Observe students and give feedback.)

EXERCISE 3

Multiplication/Addition/Subtraction

a. Look at the problems in Part 3.
- You have to add or subtract or multiply. In some of the problems you have to change numbers to fractions. In some problems you have to change mixed numbers to fractions.

b. Touch the first problem.
- What does the sign tell you to do? (Signal.) *Multiply.*
- What do you have to do first? (Signal.) *Change 3 to a fraction.*
- Do it and work the problem. ✔
- What's the answer? (Signal.) *21 eighths.*

c. Touch the next problem.

Lesson 52

- What does the sign tell you to do? (Signal.) *Add.*
- There is a mixed number in this problem. If we write that mixed number as a fraction, how many parts will be in each whole? (Signal.) *4.*
- Does the other fraction in that problem tell about the same number of parts in each whole? (Signal.) *Yes.*
- So will you be able to work the problem? (Signal.) *Yes.*
- Now you have to change the mixed number into a fraction. Next to the mixed number write the number for the parts in each whole. Then write the number on top for the wholes and parts that are left. ✔
- Figure out the fraction. (Pause.)
- What fraction does that mixed number equal? (Signal.) *9 fourths.*
- Cross out the old mixed number and finish working the problem. (Pause.)
- What's the answer to the problem? (Signal.) *12 fourths.*

d. Touch the next problem.
- What does the sign tell you to do? (Signal.) *Subtract.*
- There is a mixed number in this problem. If we write that mixed number as a fraction, how many parts will be in each whole? (Signal.) *5.*
- Does the other fraction in that problem tell about the same number of parts in each whole? (Signal.) *Yes.*
- So will you be able to work the problem? (Signal.) *Yes.*
- Now you have to change the mixed number into a fraction. Next to the mixed number write the number for the parts in each whole. Then write the number on top for the wholes and parts that are left.
- Figure out the fraction. (Pause.)
- What fraction does that mixed number equal? (Signal.) *17 fifths.*
- Cross out the old mixed number and finish working the problem. (Pause.)
- What's the answer to the problem? (Signal.) *14 fifths.*

e. Touch the next problem.
- What does the sign tell you to do? (Signal.) *Multiply.*
- This problem has a number that you change to a fraction and a mixed number that you change to a fraction. First change the number to a fraction. (Pause.)
- Now change the mixed number to a fraction. Write the number for the parts in each whole. Then write the number on top for the wholes and the parts that are left.
- Figure out the fraction. (Pause.)
- What fraction does the mixed number equal? (Signal.) *7 fourths.*
- Now finish working the problem. (Pause.)
- What's the answer? (Signal.) *21 fourths.*

f. Touch the next problem.
- What does the sign tell you to do? (Signal.) *Add.*
- If we write that mixed number as a fraction, how many parts will be in each whole? (Signal.) *2.*
- Does the other fraction in that problem tell about the same number of parts in each whole? (Signal.) *Yes.*
- So will you be able to work the problem? (Signal.) *Yes.*
- Change the mixed number into a fraction. ✔
- What fraction does that mixed number equal? (Signal.) *5 halves.*
- Now finish working the problem. (Pause.)
- What's the answer to the problem? (Signal.) *8 halves.*

g. Work the rest of the problems in Part 3. Be careful. You have 6 minutes.
- (Observe students and give feedback.)

EXERCISE 4

Workcheck

a. We're going to check the answers. Exchange workbooks, and get ready to check the answers. (Pause.)
- Put an **X** next to each problem that the person misses.
- (Check and correct. See **Answer Key.**)
- Return the workbooks.

b. Now we're going to figure out the number of points you've earned for this lesson.
- (Point to the posted information.)

Worksheet Items	Errors	Points
	0–2	10
	3	7
	4	5
	5	3
	6	1
	7 or more	0

- Count the number of items you got wrong. Figure out the number of points you earned and write the number in the "Items" box.
- (Observe students and give feedback.)

c. (Tell the group how many points they earned for the lesson.) Write that number in the "Hard Work" box; then figure out the total for today's lesson.

d. Turn to the Point Summary Charts. Write the points in the box for Lesson 52. ✔

Lesson 53

Skipping Note: Check the students' errors from Lesson 52. If no more than 1 fourth of the students made more than 4 errors, skip this lesson and proceed with Lesson 54.

EXERCISE 1

Multiplying by 1

a. Turn to Lesson 53.
- Look at the problems in Part 1.
- You have to figure out the fraction that equals 1. Touch the first problem.
- What's the bottom number you start with? (Signal.) *3.*
- What's the bottom number you end with? (Signal.) *12.*
- Tell me what you have to multiply 3 by to end with 12. Get ready. (Signal.) *4.*
- Tell me the whole fraction equal to 1 that goes in the parentheses. (Signal.) *4 fourths.*
- Write it. Then figure out the answer when you multiply. (Pause.)
- What's the answer? (Signal.) *8 twelfths.*
- You multiplied by 1, so what does the end amount equal? (Signal.) *2 thirds.*

b. Touch the next problem.
- What's the bottom number you start with? (Signal.) *2.*
- What's the bottom number you end with? (Signal.) *6.*
- Tell me what you have to multiply 2 by to end with 6. Get ready. (Signal.) *3.*
- Tell me the whole fraction equal to 1 that goes in the parentheses. (Signal.) *3 thirds.*
- Write it. Then figure out the answer when you multiply. (Pause.)
- What's the answer? (Signal.) *15 sixths.*
- You multiplied by 1, so what does the end amount equal? (Signal.) *5 halves.*

c. Touch the next problem.
- What's the bottom number you start with? (Signal.) *8.*
- What's the bottom number you end with? (Signal.) *24.*

- What do you have to multiply 8 by to end with 24? (Pause. Signal.) *3.*
- Tell me the whole fraction equal to 1 that goes in the parentheses. Get ready. (Signal.) *3 thirds.*
- Write it. Then figure out the answer when you multiply. (Pause.)
- What's the answer? (Signal.) *9/24ths.*
- You multiplied by 1, so what does the end amount equal? (Signal.) *3 eighths.*

d. Work the rest of the problems in Part 1. Figure out the fraction equal to 1, and work the problem. You have 4 minutes.
- (Observe students and give feedback.)

EXERCISE 2

Multiplication/Addition/Subtraction

a. Look at the problems in Part 2.
- You have to add or subtract or multiply. In some of the problems you have to change numbers to fractions. In some problems you have to change mixed numbers to fractions.

b. Touch the first problem.
- What does the sign tell you to do? (Signal.) *Multiply.*
- What do you have to do first? (Signal.) *Change 4 to a fraction.*
- Do it and work the problem. ✔
- What's the answer? (Signal.) *12 eighths.*

c. Touch the next problem.
- What does the sign tell you to do? (Signal.) *Add.*
- There is a mixed number in this problem. If we write that mixed number as a fraction, how many parts will be in each whole? (Signal.) *8.*
- Does the other fraction in that problem tell about the same number of parts in each whole? (Signal.) *Yes.*
- So will you be able to work the problem? (Signal.) *Yes.*

- Now you have to change the mixed number into a fraction. Next to the mixed number write the number for the parts in each whole. Then write the number on top for the wholes and parts that are left. ✔
- Figure out the fraction. (Pause.)
- What fraction does that mixed number equal? (Signal.) *11 eighths.*
- Cross out the old mixed number and finish working the problem. (Pause.)
- What's the answer to the problem? (Signal.) *17 eighths.*

d. Touch the next problem.

- What does the sign tell you to do? (Signal.) *Add.*
- There is a mixed number in this problem. If we write that mixed number as a fraction, how many parts will be in each whole? (Signal.) *5.*
- Does the other fraction in that problem tell about the same number of parts in each whole? (Signal.) *Yes.*
- So will you be able to work the problem? (Signal.) *Yes.*
- Now you have to change the mixed number into a fraction. Next to the mixed number write the number for the parts in each whole. Then write the number on top for the wholes and parts that are left. ✔
- Figure out the fraction. (Pause.)
- What fraction does that mixed number equal? (Signal.) *11 fifths.*
- Finish working the problem. (Pause.)
- What's the answer to the problem? (Signal.) *14 fifths.*

e. Touch the next problem.

- What does the sign tell you to do? (Signal.) *Multiply.*
- This problem has a number that you change to a fraction and a mixed number that you change to a fraction. First change the number to a fraction. (Pause.)
- Now change the mixed number to a fraction. Write the number for the parts in each whole. Then write the number on top for the wholes and the parts that are left. ✔
- Figure out the fraction. (Pause.)

- What fraction does the mixed number equal? (Signal.) *5 thirds.*
- Now finish working the problem. (Pause.)
- What's the answer? (Signal.) *20 thirds.*

f. Touch the next problem.

- What does the sign tell you to do? (Signal.) *Subtract.*
- If we write that mixed number as a fraction, how many parts will be in each whole? (Signal.) *4.*
- Does the other fraction in that problem tell about the same number of parts in each whole? (Signal.) *Yes.*
- So will you be able to work the problem? (Signal.) *Yes.*
- Change the mixed number into a fraction. ✔
- What fraction does that mixed number equal? (Signal.) *9 fourths.*
- Now finish working the problem. (Pause.)
- What's the answer to the problem? (Signal.) *6 fourths.*

g. Work the rest of the problems in Part 2. Be careful. You have 6 minutes.

- (Observe students and give feedback.)

EXERCISE 3

Workcheck

a. We're going to check the answers. Exchange workbooks, and get ready to check the answers. (Pause.)

- Put an **X** next to each problem that the person misses.
- (Check and correct. See **Answer Key.**)
- Return the workbooks.

b. Now we're going to figure out the number of points you've earned for this lesson.

- (Point to the posted information.)

Worksheet Items	Errors	Points
	0–2	10
	3	7
	4	5
	5	3
	6	1
	7 or more	0

- Count the number of items you got wrong. Figure out the number of points you earned and write the number in the "Items" box.
- (Observe students and give feedback.)

c. (Tell the group how many points they earned for the lesson.) Write that number in the "Hard Work" box; then figure out the total for today's lesson.

d. Turn to the Point Summary Charts. Write the points in the box for Lesson 53. ✔

Lesson 54

EXERCISE 1
Multiplying by 1

a. Turn to Lesson 54.
- Look at the problems in Part 1.
- You have to figure out the fraction that equals 1 to put in the parentheses.
- What's the bottom number you start with? (Signal.) *8.*
- What's the bottom number you end with? (Signal.) *24.*
- Tell me what you have to multiply 8 by to end with 24. Get ready. (Signal.) *3.*
- Tell me the whole fraction equal to 1 that goes in the parentheses. (Signal.) *3 thirds.*
- Write it. Then figure out the answer when you multiply. (Pause.)
- What's the answer? (Signal.) *12/24ths.*
- You multiplied by 1, so what does the end amount equal? (Signal.) *4 eighths.*

b. Touch the next problem.
- What's the bottom number you start with? (Signal.) *2.*
- What's the bottom number you end with? (Signal.) *14.*
- Tell me what you have to multiply 2 by to end with 14. Get ready. (Signal.) *7.*
- Tell me the whole fraction equal to 1 that goes in the parentheses. (Signal.) *7 sevenths.*
- Write it. Then figure out the answer when you multiply. (Pause.)
- What's the answer? (Signal.) *56/14ths.*
- You multiplied by 1, so what does the end amount equal? (Signal.) *8 halves.*

c. Work the rest of the problems in Part 1. Figure out the fraction equal to 1, and work the problem. You have 4 minutes.
- (Observe students and give feedback.)

EXERCISE 2
Multiplication/Addition/Subtraction

a. Look at the problems in Part 2.
- You have to add or subtract or multiply. In some of the problems you have to change numbers to fractions. In some problems you have to change mixed numbers to fractions.

b. Touch the first problem.
- What does the sign tell you to do? (Signal.) *Multiply.*
- What do you have to do first? (Signal.) *Change 5 to a fraction.*
- Do it and work the problem. ✔
- What's the answer? (Signal.) *20 ninths.*

c. Touch the next problem.
- What does the sign tell you to do? (Signal.) *Add.*
- There is a mixed number in this problem. If we write that mixed number as a fraction, how many parts will be in each whole? (Signal.) *3.*
- Does the other fraction in that problem tell about the same number of parts in each whole? (Signal.) *Yes.*
- So will you be able to work the problem? (Signal.) *Yes.*
- Now you have to change the mixed number into a fraction. Next to the mixed number write the number for the parts in each whole. Then write the number on top for the wholes and parts that are left. ✔
- Figure out the fraction. (Pause.)
- What fraction does that mixed number equal? (Signal.) *4 thirds.*
- Cross out the old mixed number and finish working the problem. (Pause.)
- What's the answer to the problem? (Signal.) *8 thirds.*

d. Touch the next problem.
- What does the sign tell you to do? (Signal.) *Subtract.*
- There is a mixed number in this problem. If we write that mixed number as a fraction, how many parts will be in each whole? (Signal.) *7.*

- Does the other fraction in that problem tell about the same number of parts in each whole? (Signal.) *Yes.*
- So will you be able to work the problem? (Signal.) *Yes.*
- Now you have to change the mixed number into a fraction. Next to the mixed number write the number for the parts in each whole. Then write the number on top for the wholes and parts that are left.
- Figure out the fraction. (Pause.)
- What fraction does that mixed number equal? (Signal.) *17 sevenths.*
- Finish working the problem. (Pause.)
- What's the answer to the problem? (Signal.) *8 sevenths.*

e. Touch the next problem.
- What does the sign tell you to do? (Signal.) *Multiply.*
- This problem has a number that you change to a fraction and a mixed number that you change to a fraction. First change the number to a fraction. (Pause.)
- Now change the mixed number to a fraction. Write the number for the parts in each whole. Then write the number on top for the wholes and the parts that are left.
- Figure out the fraction. (Pause.)
- What fraction does the mixed number equal? (Signal.) *8 thirds.*
- Now finish working the problem. (Pause.)
- What's the answer to the problem? (Signal.) *32 thirds.*

f. Touch the next problem.
- What does the sign tell you to do? (Signal.) *Subtract.*
- If we write that mixed number as a fraction, how many parts will be in each whole? (Signal.) *5.*
- Does the other fraction in that problem tell about the same number of parts in each whole? (Signal.) *No.*
- So will you be able to work the problem? (Signal.) *No.*
- So just skip that problem.

g. Work the rest of the problems in Part 2. Be careful. You have 6 minutes.
- (Observe students and give feedback.)

EXERCISE 3

Workcheck

a. We're going to check the answers. Exchange workbooks, and get ready to check the answers. (Pause.)
- Put an **X** next to each problem that the person misses.
- (Check and correct. See **Answer Key.**)
- Return the workbooks.

b. Now we're going to figure out the number of points you've earned for this lesson.
- (Point to the posted information.)

Worksheet Items	Errors	Points
	0–2	10
	3	7
	4	5
	5	3
	6	1
	7 or more	0

- Count the number of items you got wrong. Figure out the number of points you earned and write the number in the "Items" box.
- (Observe students and give feedback.)

c. (Tell the group how many points they earned for the lesson.) Write that number in the "Hard Work" box; then figure out the total for today's lesson.

d. Turn to the Point Summary Charts. Write the points in the box for Lesson 54. ✔

EXERCISE 1

Multiplying by 1

a. Turn to Lesson 55.
- Look at the problems in Part 1.
- You have to figure out the fraction that equals 1 to put in the parentheses.
- What's the bottom number you start with? (Signal.) *5.*
- What's the bottom number you end with? (Signal.) *30.*
- Tell me what you have to multiply 5 by to end with 30. Get ready. (Signal.) *6.*
- Tell me the whole fraction equal to 1 that goes in the parentheses. (Signal.) *6 sixths.*
- Write it. Then figure out the answer when you multiply. (Pause.)
- What's the answer? (Signal.) *48/30ths.*
- You multiplied by 1, so what does the end amount equal? (Signal.) *8 fifths.*

b. Work the rest of the problems in Part 1. Figure out the fraction equal to 1, and work the problem. You have 4 minutes.
- (Observe students and give feedback.)

EXERCISE 2

Multiplication/Addition/ Subtraction

a. Look at the problems in Part 2.
- You have to add or subtract or multiply. In some of the problems you have to change numbers to fractions. In some problems you have to change mixed numbers to fractions.

b. Touch the first problem.
- What does the sign tell you to do? (Signal.) *Multiply.*
- Do you have to change anything to a fraction first? (Signal.) *Yes.*
- What's the mixed number you have to change to a fraction? (Signal.) *1 and 3 fourths.*
- What's the number you have to change to a fraction? (Signal.) *5.*

c. Touch the next problem.

- What does the sign tell you to do? (Signal.) *Subtract.*
- Do you have to change anything to a fraction first? (Signal.) *Yes.*
- What do you have to change to a fraction? (Signal.) *2 and 3 eighths.*
- If you change that to a fraction, will you be able to work the problem? (Signal.) *No.*
- So what will you do with that problem? (Signal.) *Skip it.*

d. Touch the next problem.
- What does the sign tell you to do? (Signal.) *Add.*
- Do you have to change anything to a fraction first? (Signal.) *Yes.*
- What's the first mixed number you have to change to a fraction? (Signal.) *1 and 2 thirds.*
- What's the next mixed number you have to change to a fraction? (Signal.) *4 and 1 third.*
- Think about it. If you change those mixed numbers to fractions, will you be able to work the problem? (Pause. Signal.) *Yes.*

e. Go ahead and work the problems in Part 2. Be careful. Some problems you won't be able to work. Sometimes the problem will have 2 mixed numbers that you have to change to fractions. You have 6 minutes.
- (Observe students and give feedback.)

EXERCISE 3

Expanding Fractions

a. Touch the first problem in Part 3.
- You have to change the mixed number into a fraction.
- How many wholes do you have? (Signal.) *3.*
- So the top will be how many times bigger than the bottom? (Signal.) *3.*

b. Touch the next problem.
- There is a number you have to write as a fraction.
- What will you write? (Signal.) *4 over 1.*

c. Touch the next problem.

- There is a fraction you have to write as a number.
- What's the bottom number? (Signal.) *4.*
- How many times bigger than 4 is the top?(Signal.) *5.*
d. Do the problems in Part 3. Write a number for each fraction. Write a fraction for each number and each mixed number. You have 3 minutes.
- (Observe students and give feedback.)

EXERCISE 4

Workcheck

a. We're going to check the answers. Exchange workbooks, and get ready to check the answers. (Pause.)
- Put an **X** next to each problem that the person misses.
- (Check and correct. See **Answer Key.**)
- Return the workbooks.
b. Now we're going to figure out the number of points you've earned for this lesson.
- (Point to the posted information.)

Worksheet Items	Errors	Points
	0–2	10
	3	7
	4	5
	5	3
	6	1
	7 or more	0

- Count the number of items you got wrong. Figure out the number of points you earned and write the number in the "Items" box.
- (Observe students and give feedback.)
c. (Tell the group how many points they earned for the lesson.) Write that number in the "Hard Work" box; then figure out the total for today's lesson.
d. Turn to the Point Summary Charts. Write the points in the box for Lesson 55. ✔
e. Total your points for Lessons 51 through 55 and write the total number on the chart.
- (Observe students and give feedback.)
f. Everybody, find the Five-Lesson Point Graph. ✔
- (Help the students plot their five-lesson scores on the graph.)

Basic Fractions Pretest Part 1   Name _____

Part A

2	7	4	2	4	1	7	4	2	7
+ 4	+ 6	+ 2	+ 5	+ 1	+ 8	+ 8	+ 3	+ 8	+ 7

$4 + 9 =$ $3 + 2 =$ $5 + 1 =$ $3 + 8 =$ $5 + 7 =$

$9 + 6 =$ $3 + 5 =$ $6 + 4 =$ $4 + 7 =$ $1 + 9 =$

9	2	1	3	9	5	6	7	5	4
+ 4	+ 2	+ 5	+ 1	+ 1	+ 8	+ 3	+ 3	+ 9	+ 4

Part B

6	7	6	5	1	10	7	8	10	5
− 4	− 6	− 2	− 1	− 0	− 8	− 3	− 5	− 7	− 3

$9 - 6 =$ $6 - 1 =$ $9 - 8 =$ $10 - 5 =$ $10 - 9 =$

$5 - 2 =$ $4 - 3 =$ $8 - 3 =$ $9 - 7 =$ $6 - 4 =$

4	4	10	9	7	8	7	8	8	8
− 2	− 1	− 6	− 3	− 5	− 7	− 4	− 4	− 6	− 1

Part C

$1 \times 3 =$ $6 \times 5 =$ $1 \times 8 =$ $4 \times 5 =$ $5 \times 3 =$ $5 \times 5 =$

$4 \times 1 =$ $4 \times 6 =$ $2 \times 1 =$ $6 \times 2 =$ $1 \times 5 =$ $4 \times 8 =$

$3 \times 2 =$ $2 \times 9 =$ $5 \times 6 =$ $3 \times 7 =$ $3 \times 6 =$ $6 \times 7 =$

$6 \times 3 =$ $5 \times 8 =$ $4 \times 3 =$ $5 \times 2 =$ $6 \times 4 =$ $2 \times 6 =$

$3 \times 5 =$ $5 \times 5 =$ $2 \times 4 =$ $6 \times 9 =$ $2 \times 4 =$ $3 \times 9 =$

Copyright © SRA/McGraw-Hill. Permission is granted to reproduce for classroom use.

Basic Fractions Pretest Part 2   Name _____

Part D

$\dfrac{3}{5} + \dfrac{9}{5} =$ $\dfrac{3}{4} + \dfrac{3}{4} =$ $\dfrac{8}{7} + \dfrac{5}{7} =$

$\dfrac{7}{6} - \dfrac{5}{6} =$ $\dfrac{10}{3} + \dfrac{6}{3} =$ $\dfrac{5}{3} - \dfrac{2}{3} =$

Part E

$\dfrac{3}{4} \times \dfrac{7}{6} =$ $\dfrac{1}{6} \times \dfrac{4}{6} =$ $\dfrac{5}{4} \times \dfrac{2}{6} =$

$\dfrac{4}{3} \times \dfrac{8}{5} =$ $\dfrac{3}{4} \times \dfrac{4}{5} =$ $\dfrac{3}{2} \times \dfrac{7}{8} =$

Part F

$1\dfrac{3}{8} + \dfrac{7}{8} =$ $4\dfrac{1}{2} \times 1\dfrac{3}{4} =$ $1\dfrac{1}{3} - \dfrac{2}{3} =$

$2\dfrac{1}{4} - \dfrac{3}{4} =$ $2\dfrac{1}{3} \times 4 =$ $\dfrac{4}{5} + 2\dfrac{1}{5} =$

Copyright © SRA/McGraw-Hill. Permission is granted to reproduce for classroom use.

Basic Fractions Pretest Error Chart

Name	Errors					
	A	**B**	**C**	**D**	**E**	**F**